$\mathcal{W}$ interthur's heritage is deeply rooted in a commitment to preservation and education. The museum's program in art conservation has provided an unparalleled training ground for experts in the field, many of whom are currently responsible for the restoration of significant works of historical and national interest.

In this book, the talented Winterthur conservators share their extensive knowledge as well as the lessons they have learned in caring for one of the world's leading decorative arts collections.

Likewise, our knowledge of art, antiques, and collectibles goes back more than one hundred years. Whatever the collection—photographs, decorative arts, memorabilia, or fine art—more likely than not, it's insured by Chubb. Support of this book, and more importantly of Winterthur, is only logical for Chubb.

We hope that you find this book helpful in preserving your most cherished items for future generations.

Compliments of Your Friends at the

CHUBB GROUP OF INSURANCE COMPANIES

THE WINTERTHUR GUIDE TO
Caring for Your Collection

GREGORY J. LANDREY

KATE DUFFY

JANICE CARLSON

LOIS OLCOTT PRICE

BRUNO P. POULIOT

MARGARET A. LITTLE

LINDA EATON

DEBRA HESS NORRIS

JOHN KRILL

BETTY FISKE

MARK F. BOCKRATH

MICHAEL S. PODMANICZKY

MARY C. PETERSON

HENRY FRANCIS DU PONT WINTERTHUR MUSEUM
WINTERTHUR, DELAWARE

DISTRIBUTED BY UNIVERSITY PRESS OF NEW ENGLAND
HANOVER AND LONDON

SERIES EDITOR: *Onie Rollins*

CONTENT EDITOR: *Onie Rollins*

COPY EDITOR: *Teresa A. Vivolo*

DESIGNER: *Abby Goldstein*

ે૧

The Winterthur Guide to Caring for Your Collections
was generously supported by
CHUBB GROUP OF INSURANCE COMPANIES

ે૧

LIBRARY OF CONGRESS CATALOGING-IN-PUBLICATION DATA

The Winterthur guide to caring for your collection/
Gregory J. Landrey...[et al.].
p. cm. – (Winterthur decorative arts series)
Includes bibliographical references.

ISBN 0-912724-52-8

1. Henry Francis du Pont Winterthur Museum.
2. Art – Conservation and restoration – Delaware – Winterthur.
I. Landrey, Gregory J. II. Henry Francis du Pont Winterthur Museum. III. Series.

N5220.H494 W56   2000
702'.8'8–dc21

00-040794
CIP

TABLE OF CONTENTS

INTRODUCTION

GREGORY J. LANDREY

$\mathcal{E}$ach of us can probably recollect some item from our past, once loved, now lost or feared lost, whether to time, the elements, or carelessness. Are any of the following scenarios familiar to you?

- *An enthusiastic trip to the attic to find a family heirloom turns bleak. You discover the old silver teapot but instantly become discouraged as you observe how black and tarnished it is. Is it possible to regain the teapot's former gleam? What is the best way to polish it without causing harm?*

- *Good fortune befalls you at a country auction, where you are the successful bidder on an eighteenth-century candlestand. Once you see it in good light, however, you are dismayed to find that the finish on the top is seriously blemished. Can anything be done with this great find that otherwise has such potential?*

- *An old oil painting that you bought at an antiques store is so dark that you wonder if maybe it would benefit from being "restored." What would that entail?*

- *The stitching holding together a Civil War diary that was passed along to you from your great-uncle is coming apart. Are there ways to preserve it while still keeping it accessible?*

In countless scenarios every day, we are met with the opportunity to care for and even preserve the things that we value, whether they are personal collections, family heirlooms, or simply things that we hold dear. *The Winterthur Guide to Caring for Your Collection* addresses questions and scenarios such as those above—and more, giving you guidelines and techniques on how to properly care for your treasures. Written by museum professionals and from a conservation perspective, this book offers practical solutions to problems that you might encounter.

What is meant by this word *conservation? Conservation* denotes a manner of care or treatment where the goal is to repair damage if present, while taking action to prevent or retard further deterioration of an object. You may be more familiar with the term *restoration,* which refers to a manner of care or treatment where the goal is to bring an object back as close as possible to its original appearance or function. Although restoration can be a part of the care and treatment of an object, it is a subset of the umbrella term *conservation.* Both of the terms come into play with each of the examples given above. For instance, removing tarnish from the silver teapot, or restoring "its former gleam," can be done in a variety of ways. It is best carried out, however, within the context of preventing further deterioration, that is, with its *conservation* in mind.

This book focuses primarily on the conservation of objects, where the goals are minimizing change and maximizing longevity. It presents a lucid approach to the practical skills of conservation—what to do and what *not* to do. Only momentary reflection is necessary to see the inherent problems of an uninformed approach to the care of ones' treasured objects. Critical information can be lost and an object permanently damaged when things are cared for without basic guidelines and information. Overzealous treatment of the antique candlestand may result in the loss of desirable evidence of age and use. Using the wrong materials in treating the finish could harm the wood itself. A treatment choice for the darkened oil painting could result in an unwanted change that could not be undone. Problems such as these can result from ignoring a central tenet of conservation, which is to make what you do as reversible as possible.

What each of us does individually for the care and conservation of our personal possessions or collections is not an isolated activity. It is part of a much broader effort to protect objects of personal, historical, and artistic importance from premature demise. There are several professional organizations dedicated to just this cause (see Professional Organizations). Each of the following chapters puts forth guidelines to help you determine when the solution to a problem is likely to be beyond the skills of the average collector and when to seek professional advice. Local museums are often a good first contact. They can refer you to other professional organizations and conservators. Also, the American Institute for Conservation in Washington, D.C., has brochures and a referral system to help you

make contact with the right professional. The best advice you can follow is to consult a professional if you have any doubts.

We enjoy the things that we have collected as well as those that have been passed
down to us through our families. Acquiring the skills and knowledge to properly
care for such items and thus ensure their preservation is an attainable goal. Who
knows? Your great-uncle's Civil War diary may well be a museum or library artifact
some day, prized as an irreplaceable treasure for the unique information it contains.
Or it may become the cherished possession of your great-grandchildren. But these
things can happen only if good judgment and care are exercised now.

Fig. 1. Granddaughter's Bedroom, Corbit-Sharp House, Historic Houses of Odessa

CHAPTER I

General Care

GREGORY J. LANDREY WITH ROBERT W. HOAG

*T*he general care of objects is primarily a matter of common sense. Creating an ideal environment is the first priority *(fig. 1)*. This includes controlling light exposure, avoiding environmental extremes, and keeping display areas clean. These basic preventive measures, discussed below, are necessary to inhibit deterioration and will do much to prolong the life of your cherished treasures.

Light

One of the more life-giving steps you can take toward the long-term preservation of your collection is to control the light that your objects are subjected to. While it is by light that we are able to see the things we value, light is also a major player in their demise. Both the visible and ultraviolet (UV) components of light are responsible. Certainly this is not new information. The damaging effects of light have long been known. For that very reason, generations of housekeepers have covered furnishings with sheets when a room was vacant. Indeed, light is particularly damaging to furnishings and to colored surfaces and finishes—and more specifically to things made from organic materials, such as paper, fabric, wood, and leather *(fig. 2)*. Realistically, it is not possible to wholly eliminate light damage. However, modest steps can be taken to manage light so that objects do not prematurely deteriorate.

Fig. 2. The rich color of this eighteenth-century resist-dyed blue-on-white linen upholstery from a chair seat has suffered severe damage due to exposure to sunlight. One side of the seat (at top in photo) has faded the most, as it was closest to the light source.

Carefully considered object placement is perhaps the first and most common-sense solution to managing light exposure. Since most objects are at least at some risk when exposed to direct sunlight, display locations for valued objects should be out of the sun's direct daily path.

Reducing the amount of sunlight coming into an area is the next logical consideration. This can be accomplished in a variety of ways. The regular use of blinds, shades, curtains, and shutters is extremely effective in canceling the harmful effects of daylight. Their use *does* require discipline on the owner's part, however, since they are of no value if they are not closed at the appropriate times.

Daylight can also be controlled right at the source of entry—the window. Most window retailers are equipped to discuss options for daylight control. These include the application of filters on existing windows to reduce the amount of light coming in or new or replacement windows that reduce levels of ultraviolet and visible-light transmission. Glass specified with a low "E" rating, for example, reduces the amount of ultraviolet light transmission. Separate tinted storm windows or glazing materials applied directly to glass also reduce the sun's damaging rays. Practical considerations, such as the brightness of the window to the outside world, need to be balanced with the desire to safeguard your collection; but no matter which options are selected, be sure to limit daylight exposure, particularly with objects that are made of, or colored with, organic materials.

❧ *Artificial Light*

Artificial light can be a problem for sensitive materials as well. Dimmers and appropriate-wattage bulbs can be useful tools in managing artificial light exposure. You should determine the minimum amount of light needed to appreciate an object and stop at that point. Be aware that tungsten, halogen, and even fluorescent bulbs generate a lot of heat, which in turn speeds up the chemical mechanisms of deterioration. This is particularly true when lights are used in closed display cabinets. Keep objects a safe distance from any light source to limit both light and heat exposure.

❧ *Monitoring and Measuring Light Exposure*

Light exposure is measured in units of energy. Light levels can be stated in terms of "footcandles" (a unit of light produced by one candela at a distance of one foot, or, the amount of light equal to one lumen per square foot) or "lux" (an international measurement of light equal to one lumen per square meter). One footcandle equals approximately 10 lux. A handheld light meter that generates information in either footcandles or lux is the quickest way to establish the amount of light to which an object has been exposed. The Light Exposure Standards chart can be used as a general guide for suggested limits of exposure for various types of objects. Remember, it is the overall long-term exposure or cumulative effect that matters, not necessarily the momentary measurement. Full daylight exposure of a textile at 3,000 lux for one hour will cause as much damage as 100 hours at 30 lux. Various types of light-registering equipment units are used by collectors and in museums to establish long-term exposure data (see List of Suppliers). This information can then be used for light control procedures. Keep it simple. Work with what resources and display opportunities you have to eliminate excessive light exposure.

☙   *Temperature and Humidity*

Our personal comfort is usually motivation enough to see that our work areas and homes are properly heated and cooled. The motivation for creating a stable environment for objects is another matter. Most organic materials expand and contract as temperature and relative humidity swing up and down. These fluctuations cause unwanted changes to objects, such as splitting and distortion. In addition, high levels of humidity may lead to mold growth. The degradation of organic materials is accelerated with increased temperature. The projected useful "life" of a rare book may be cut in half with every 10°F increase in temperature. Taking reasonable steps to control temperature and humidity will go a long way toward preserving our collections for future generations.

Proper temperature and relative humidity maintenance in collection areas simply means avoiding the extremes of both. In addition, rapid changes in temperature and relative humidity can be detrimental. While museums typically try to maintain a temperature of approximately 72°F and 50 percent relative humidity, this is rarely possible for personal collections. The following guidelines are worth keeping in mind, however.

A relative humidity between 40 and 60 percent is generally appropriate for most collections. The following chapters will include additional specifications for certain types of objects. Mold growth can develop above 70 percent, and excessive dehydration may result below 30 percent. The "40–60" rule protects you from getting too close to the range where problems may develop. Keeping temperatures in the moderate range is also important. Condensation on objects may occur in some climates below 50°F, and the rate of degradation will increase as a room temperature of 72°F is exceeded. Storing family photographs in an unventilated attic is a sure way to hurry their deterioration and ensure that your grandchildren will see damaged images of their ancestors, if they see them at all. Again, for most collections, it is best to avoid the extremes—typically those that you will find in attics and basements.

A fully integrated heating, ventilating, and air conditioning (HVAC) system regulates both temperature and relative humidity and is the best aid in creating a stable environment for your collection. When private residences do not have HVAC systems in place, supplemental systems are in order. Humidifiers and dehumidifiers can help if they are properly monitored. Fans, to keep air circulating, are valuable as well. There are a variety of techniques and equipment to help you determine if you have the right environmental conditions. These range from inexpensive cards that give humidity readings *(fig. 3)* to expensive temperature and humidity-measuring units. Suppliers for reliable monitoring systems are listed in the List of Suppliers.

৯   *Dust*

Keep your collection as dust-free as possible. Not only will the objects appear better cared for if dusted, but they will, in fact, also be in a better state of long-term preservation. Dust is made up of many things, including air pollutants such as sulfur and carbon, as well as hair, skin, and lint. Its vices are numerous. Because it is hygroscopic by nature, meaning that it attracts and retains moisture, dust is a breeding ground for mold. It can also attract insects. Further, it may encourage corrosion, speeding up the tarnishing of metals.

There are a number of things that can be done to limit dust exposure. Proper filtering of heating and air conditioning systems; the placement of appropriate objects in acid-free boxes, in glass or acrylic cases, or in other object-specific enclosures; and dusting are all critical steps in collection care.

Objects that are displayed in the open should be dusted regularly. Dusting is a specific task that should not be confused with polishing. In fact, it should always be performed separately from the specialized activity of polishing. In dusting, the objective is solely to remove the dust without leaving any other deposits behind. Polishing actually causes a change to the surface of an object (see chapter 8, "Metals," and chapter 11, "Furniture," for more on polishing).

Dusting can be completed successfully with a variety of cloths and equipment. The options include commercial cloths treated to collect dust; dry and lint-free dust cloths; dust attractants marketed to be applied to dust cloths; long, fine-bristle brushes; and

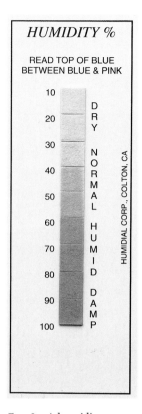

FIG. 3. A humidity indicator card is an inexpensive way to monitor relative humidity. The boundary between pink and blue indicates the relative humidity. This card indicates a relative humidity of approximately 40%. These cards are available through suppliers listed in the List of Suppliers.

vacuum cleaners. Some dust cloths are charged with static electricity to hold the dust while others are treated with dust-attractant chemicals. You can test the effectiveness of a dust cloth by dusting a windowpane. Does the cloth remove and retain the dust? Does it leave the glass otherwise unchanged? A "yes" answer to these questions suggests that you have an effective dusting cloth. Does the dust remain behind or become dispersed to the air? Does the duster cause the test surface to become oily in any way? Positive responses to these questions indicate that the duster is inappropriate for use on your collection or treasures.

Be aware that some surfaces are too fragile to be dusted safely, such as those with flaking paint or gilding that is lifting off. A careful examination of objects is wise before you set out on a dusting campaign. Long, fine-bristle brushes are particularly effective on fragile surfaces and in hard-to-reach areas, both of which are present on objects such as ornate, gilded frames. Choose a brush with the softest bristles. It is best to dust from the object onto a dusting cloth rather than letting the dust float into the air, where it may be redeposited on other objects nearby.

Vacuum cleaners are a more powerful approach to removing dust, but they must be used carefully. A standard household vacuum cleaner will work well on floors and around furniture. However, a system with controllable suction should be used on fragile objects, such as aged upholstery and rugs. A nylon mesh screen placed over the vacuum intake can prevent material from being sucked up and can reduce the risk of abrasion. Specialized vacuum cleaners are equipped with HEPA (High Efficiency Particulate Air) filters capable of blocking very small particles. Other vacuums operate with a water filter to fully clean the air. Manufacturers' information can be used to select the vacuum most suitable for your needs. Whether you choose a standard vacuum cleaner or one with a specialized collection and filtering system, remember that regular vacuuming is vital for both dust and insect control.

Pests

The word *pest* generally refers to rodents, birds, insects, and other types of animal life that pose a threat to the objects in your care. Taking measures to keep pests out of a space is an obvious but often overlooked precaution. Along with lighting and dust control, reducing the risk of pest damage to vulnerable collections is critical.

Storage areas such as attics and basements are often subject to unwanted visitors in the form of mice, birds, and worse *(fig. 4)*. And insects can wreak havoc.

Silverfish can destroy paper objects, and powder post beetles will devour wood structures. Some insects will find sufficient protein to sustain life from accumulated dust. Others lay eggs in dead insect carcasses.

What can be done to discourage pest damage and to limit insect life in the proximity of your collection? Maintaining proper collection hygiene, as mentioned above, is the first and most important step in pest control. Keeping food away from collections may be difficult for some domestic collections; however, creating unnecessary food debris, such as eating snacks while going through your old photograph collection, is asking for trouble. A clean area is the first line of defense. Using appropriate containers rather than shoeboxes to store nondisplay items, such as grandmother's neatly folded love letters, can save you the disappointment of finding tattered paper fragments recognizable only as a mouse nest. Metal and plastic units are readily available and can help keep objects from getting soiled or chewed (see List of Suppliers).

Working with a professional pest control service is the most effective way to maintain a pest-free collection area. It is best to find a firm that will seek to control all forms of animal life that are a potential risk for your collections.

FIG. 4. This interior view of a cupboard drawer, dating from circa 1800, depicts how much damage a rodent inflicted upon an object. Controlling pests, whether mice, squirrels, or carpet beetles, is a critical part of caring for collections.

๑   *Moving*

Inevitably, objects need to be moved. Whether you are moving them cross-country or across town, make sure that appropriate packing materials and supports (as outlined throughout this book) are used and that they are as inert, or chemically stable, as possible. While the average cardboard box may be fine for moving some things, it is not inert and should be avoided for your collection items and personal treasures—particularly if the contents are to remain in storage for some time. Acid-free tissue paper is a useful buffer for many objects. It can be used as padding and as an isolation layer from other packing materials. When packing older treasures, consider them inherently fragile, requiring extra-special care. For specific questions, consult a conservator. Art handlers can also provide valuable guidance for packing and moving a collection. Local museums are often a good resource for guidance with art handling matters.

๑   *Working with a Conservator*

Despite the very best of care given by individual collectors, it is inevitable that objects will need the attention of a professional. But how do you find the appropriate person? The process of selecting a conservator is similar to the one you may go through in choosing any other professional. You need to be sure that their specific skills are a good match for the job at hand. Conservators are required to hold certain professional standards as the basis for their work. Primary among them is to preserve the object by first seeking to stop sources of degradation. Treatments are to be as reversible as possible, meaning that any work on the object can be undone in the future without detrimentally affecting any part of the original. Some procedures may be highly reversible, while other treatments can be very difficult to undo. However, both may be appropriate. Conservators, therefore, should be expected to present a proposal for work to be done as well as a report on the completion of the treatment. This will ensure that you are fully apprised of the extent of work done to your object. Be sure to obtain before-and-after photo documentation also. Finally, look for a conservator who is affiliated with a professional organization or other conservators. Choosing a conservator by following these guidelines will help you find the right match of professional and object. While it is important to select a conservator with care, it is also worthwhile to stay in touch throughout the project. A mark of a good conservator is his or her interest in working closely with the owner and encouraging the owner to stay involved in the treatment process. The activity of conserving objects that are important to us can be a fascinating, enjoyable, and rewarding experience.

Approaching the care of our collections with some common sense and a commitment to preservation will do much to increase our long-term enjoyment of them.

LIGHT EXPOSURE STANDARDS

MATERIAL	ANNUAL LIGHT EXPOSURE NOT TO EXCEED
HIGHLY SENSITIVE ORGANIC MATERIALS particularly vulnerable textiles, paper, dyes	50,000 LH, 50 KLH, OR .05 MLH 14 LUX x 10 HOURS x 365 DAYS = APPROX. 50,000 LUX HOURS
SENSITIVE ORGANIC MATERIALS textiles, paper, dyes	180,000 LH, 180 KLH, OR .18 MLH 50 LUX x 10 HOURS x 365 DAYS = APPROX. 180,000 LUX HOURS
MODERATELY SENSITIVE ORGANIC MATERIALS WOOD, OIL PAINT	730,000 LH, 730 KLH, OR .73 MLH 200 LUX x 10 HOURS x 365 DAYS = APPROX. 730,000 LUX HOURS

Both ultraviolet and visible light can be damaging to collection objects and need to be controlled. The above standards state the total annual light exposure permissible for Winterthur's collections. Achieving these standards does not eliminate light damage to collection objects. These standards are a compromise between seeking to preserve the object while allowing sufficient light for viewing. These figures do take into consideration the law of reciprocity, which states that it is the total exposure (illuminance and time) that matters. As an example, a room with sensitive organic materials could be maintained at a low light level of 30 lux when not on view (7 hours per day) and 85 lux when guests are in the room (3 hours per day). The net exposure in this example would still be within the above standards for sensitive materials.

30 LUX x 7 HOURS x 365 DAYS	=	76,650 LH
85 LUX x 3 HOURS x 365 DAYS	=	93,075 LH
TOTAL ANNUAL EXPOSURE	=	APPROX. 170,000 LH
1 LUX	=	1 LUMEN PER SQUARE METER
1 FOOTCANDLE	=	1 LUMEN PER SQUARE FOOT
1 FOOTCANDLE	=	10 LUX
LH	=	LUX HOUR
KLH	=	KILOLUX-HOURS
MLH	=	MEGALUX-HOURS

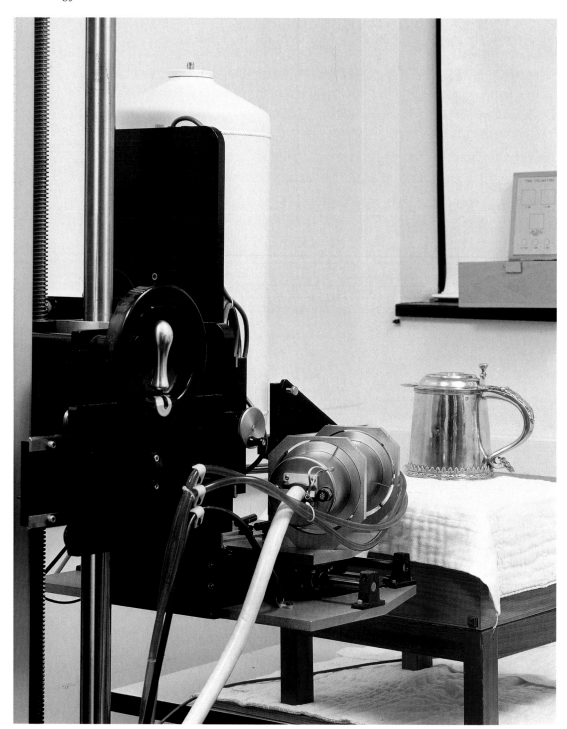

Fig. 1. A typical setup of an X-ray tube from an X-ray fluorescence (XRF) analyzer used for nondestructive elemental analysis. X rays are directed toward the surface of the object, in this case a tankard, which then produces its own X rays that are in turn collected by a detector and transferred electronically to a computer system for display and interpretation.

CHAPTER 2

Science and Your Collection

KATE DUFFY AND JANICE CARLSON

*A*n important adjunct to caring for your collection is the identification of the materials used in the creation or manufacture of the objects. Questions might include: What are the pigments used on this painting, and are they consistent with the artist's working dates? Is the silver alloy in this teapot consistent with colonial American silver? Is the coating on this object a modern synthetic, or is it "natural" and "old"? The answers to these questions may also help in determining the object's place and time of origin—that is, its authenticity.

Museum scientists use a myriad of tools to chemically and physically examine an art object. The sophisticated analytical instrumentation is taken from the research and industrial worlds but is slightly modified for specific museum applications *(fig. 1)*. This chapter will introduce you to some of the techniques available and provide you with an understanding of what information can and cannot be discovered by scientific analysis of artistic and historic objects.

It is important to remember that the first and most important step in the analytical process is consultation with a museum scientist. Such a discussion will help define what exactly you are hoping to learn, whether and how the question(s) can be addressed, whether reasonable answers are possible, and, in general, what to expect. Additionally, you will gain a clear idea of the costs and probable outcome and can then make an informed decision whether and how to proceed.

> ୬ *Nature of the Technology*

DATING:

Two broad categories of analysis exist for use in authentication studies. The first is dating—assigning a probable date or range of dates for the fabrication of an object. Three techniques can provide a "specific" date range for objects from pre-historic to medieval times: carbon dating, dendrochronology, and thermolumine-cent dating.

CARBON-14: Carbon-14 (C-14), a radioactive isotope of elemental carbon (carbon-12), is produced in the upper atmosphere and is "taken up" by plants, which "end up" in animals. This constant cycle results in an equilibrium ratio of radioactive carbon-14 to carbon-12 in living organisms. Once an organism dies, no new C-14 is added, and the remaining bit dissipates. Scientists can measure the remaining C-14 to determine age. This technique is useful for objects that are anywhere from 500 to 35,000 years old. It is not particularly helpful in dating objects less than about 500 years old.

DENDROCHRONOLOGY: Dendrochronology is a second type of dating. In this method, the number and width of tree rings in a section of wood—such as a panel painting or furniture object—are compared to the patterns obtained from estab-lished tree-ring data. By observing these patterns, it is possible for scientists to deter-mine when a tree was felled and, hence, the earliest possible date for the wood in an object—although they cannot necessarily determine when that wood might have been used to create an object. Data banks of tree-ring patterns are well established for certain northern and central European wood varieties (oak, beech, and some conifers) and time periods (the thirteenth to nineteenth centuries), but patterns are not well established for other species or periods.

THERMOLUMINESCENCE: Thermoluminescence, a third dating technique, is used exclusively for ceramics and clays. With this technique, a tiny sample of clay is drilled from a ceramic object or removed from the core of a cast metal object. The clay particles contain crystalline lattice sites, or holes, that trap energy in the form of electrons. When the clay material is heated, that energy is released in a form of light called thermoluminescence. By detecting and plotting the amount of "light" that is emitted, an object's approximate age can be determined.

Dating techniques can be applied to objects that span the millennia, representing human accomplishments throughout history in all parts of the world. When dealing with Americana—objects from the seventeenth through twentieth centuries—the time span is much more focused, and the three dating techniques described above are of little use. Instead, dating or authenticating relatively recent objects becomes a sleuthing process—through inferential analysis.

INFERENTIAL ANALYSIS:

Using instrumental techniques, an object's materials are identified, and the results are compared to a body of established knowledge. It should be stressed that authentication by this method is less definitive than established dating techniques. The scientist can offer only a statement of fact gathered from the analysis and, if possible, place that analytical data in a historical context. Additional discussion among the owner, the scientist, the art historian or curator, and the conservator will lead to the most complete understanding of the object.

While the questions asked by collectors are often similar—"What is this object made of?" or "How old is this object?"—the analytical means to the answers will differ significantly depending on the medium. For example, a collector of seventeenth-century paintings would not require the same information as a collector of nineteenth-century silver soup tureens. An initial meeting with a museum scientist/analyst is essential to establish the proper route of examination. Discussion prior to an analysis will help eliminate needless tests and can save money and time.

There are two basic types of analysis: nondestructive (nonsampling) and destructive (sampling). Sampling, as the name implies, requires removing a scraping, a drilling, or a tiny fragment from an object. The sample in many cases is very small—invisible to the naked eye. Nondestructive analysis can be carried out in several ways.

Nondestructive (Nonsampling) Analysis: Energy Dispersive X-ray Fluorescence: One of the most widely used techniques for nondestructive analysis is X-ray fluorescence (XRF), in which a two-to six-millimeter diameter X-ray beam is focused on the surface of an object, causing the elements in the surface to produce their own characteristic fluorescent X rays—an identifiable fingerprint. The elements detected in the surface of the object are displayed on a computer screen as an energy spectrum (fig. 2).

FIG. 2. This XRF spectrum shows the presence of mercury and lead in an area of red paint from the surface of a painted box. The presence of mercury indicates the use of vermilion (mercury sulfide) and lead white. Both pigments have been in common use for many centuries. Their presence here confirms the use of historic pigments but does not indicate when those pigments were applied.

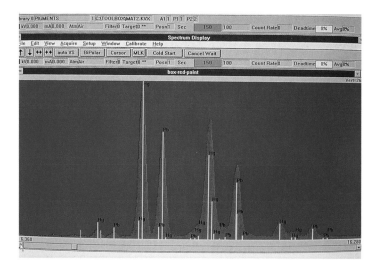

XRF analysis identifies the chemical elements present in the area of the object that is being analyzed. Pigments in watercolor or oil paintings, metal alloys, pottery, and glass can all be examined for elemental content by XRF. In some cases, depending upon the computer programs associated with each specific instrument, the elemental results can be quantified. That is, both the presence of elements (qualitative analysis) and the amount or concentration of each element (quantitative analysis) can be determined.

XRF and Paintings: Often a painting cannot be sampled for pigment identification, yet the owner would like a list of the pigments used in its creation. XRF can help. For example, if a red paint area is analyzed and the resultant spectrum contains mercury and lead, the presence of vermilion (a mercuric sulfide) and red or white lead is strongly suggested. The information gathered through XRF becomes important when the elements that are identified represent pigments that are inconsistent with the attributed date of the painting. For example, questions may arise when titanium is identified on a painting supposedly created in the late 1800s. The presence of titanium throughout a painting strongly suggests the presence of titanium dioxide—a pigment that was not commercially available to artists until after 1914. It is possible that the titanium-containing areas could be the result of retouching that was done in the twentieth century. However, if no restoration is evident, the XRF data strongly indicates that the painting was created after 1914 rather than in the late 1800s.

XRF and Metals: XRF can be used in the identification and quantification of elements in silver objects and thus aid in dating the objects and in determining their geographic origin. The analytical lab at Winterthur has an immense database of XRF silver analysis that includes data for American, British, and some Continental silver. This data provides the basis for the comparative analysis of other silver alloy objects. For example, it has been determined that from the fourteenth century on, British silversmiths adhered to the silver sterling standard of 92.5 percent silver. American silversmiths, however, were not legally bound to any compositional standard until about 1906. As a result, British silver nearly always meets or exceeds the sterling standard whereas American-made silver frequently does not. Such information allows scientists or analysts to distinguish between silver from these two regions.

In addition, knowing the silver content of an object aids greatly in assigning a date to that object. For example, much of the silver made in America prior to the early twentieth century contains approximately 86.0 to 90.0 percent pure silver. Other components of the alloy are copper (8 to 14 percent) and small amounts (less than 0.1 percent) of gold and lead. Traces of gold and lead are routinely found in silver refined before the mid nineteenth century; thus, their presence or absence is an indicator of relative age. Modern refining techniques, developed in the mid nineteenth century, made it possible to eliminate trace "contaminants" such as gold and lead. Therefore, the absence of these elements in an object is strong evidence that the silver in the object was refined after about 1850 and that the object was fabricated after that date as well.

A silver tankard that was attributed on the basis of its maker's mark to Joseph Richardson, a prominent late eighteenth-century Philadelphia silversmith, was quantitatively analyzed at Winterthur by XRF in several different areas *(fig. 3)*. The lid and the handle were found to contain at least 92.5 percent silver (suggesting a British origin) with a small amount of lead and gold. The body of the tankard contains 92.5 percent silver, with 7.5 percent copper—modern sterling silver *(fig. 4)*. Neither gold nor lead were detected in the body, indicating that it contains silver that was refined after the mid nineteenth century. The sterling content of other parts, however, together with the fact that these parts contain trace amounts of gold and lead, do indicate an object with an eighteenth-century British origin—but also one whose body has been replaced using twentieth-century silver.

Right and below:

FIGS. 3, 4. Nondestructive XRF analysis shows that the body of this eighteenth-century British tankard was replaced with modern sterling silver. The XRF spectra of the tankard side shows it to be made of modern sterling silver containing 92.5 percent silver and 7.5 percent copper. The silver content of the lid and handle is greater than 92.5, however, and these parts also contain trace amounts of gold and lead—typical of silver refined prior to the mid nineteenth century. Such a discovery helped scientists and curators determine that this tankard was altered after the mid nineteenth century.

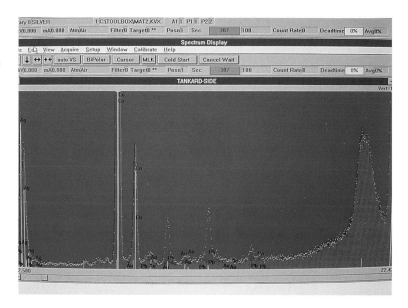

XRF and Glass: Glass is another medium that benefits from XRF analysis. Some of the major components of glass—such as the lead in lead glass as well as the metal oxides added to molten glass to produce various colors or other properties— can be identified. For example, the appearance of cobalt in the XRF spectrum of a blue glass suggests that cobalt oxide was added as a coloring agent; manganese detected in a purple glass reflects the use of manganese oxide to produce the purple color. Iron is often identified in dark green glass; it might have been present in the raw materials or deliberately added to the molten glass to achieve a certain color.

XRF analysis can also be applied to authentication studies of glass, as is the case with Amelung objects *(fig. 5)*. John Frederick Amelung was an eighteenth-century glassmaker who emigrated from Germany after the Revolutionary War and settled in Frederick County, Maryland. He set up the New Bremen Glass Works and produced common tableware as well as elaborate, colorless wares that were given as presentation pieces to dignitaries. Amelung had his own recipe for colorless glass that included the addition of antimony salts to remove bubbles that would otherwise detract from the clear glass. Elemental analysis of the signed or otherwise well-documented Amelung pieces (as well as glass shards found at the site of the original glassworks) has resulted in the identification of a uniform recipe, including a consistent level of antimony. In any questionable situation, glass objects thought to have come from the Amelung shop can be analyzed by XRF and the results compared to those from authenticated pieces.

X-Radiography: X-radiography is a technique often used in the field of conservation to examine the structural makeup of paintings, metals, ceramics, and stone objects. The equipment in many museums is similar to that used in hospitals to detect broken bones. In the museum world, for example, an X ray may reveal the presence of a blind crack that might not otherwise be detected in a ceramic vase. X rays also help in detecting manufacturing clues. X rays of furniture can reveal what type of drill bits were used in the construction of a piece, thus aiding in the dating of objects. For example, an X ray of a chair that reveals the characteristic mark of a late nineteenth-century drill bit would certainly call into question the authenticity of that piece if it were dated to the eighteenth century.

X-radiography of paintings can be helpful in determining a painting's nature and condition. Since the degree of X-ray absorption varies depending upon the chemical makeup of the pigment used, it is possible to distinguish some pigments by dif-

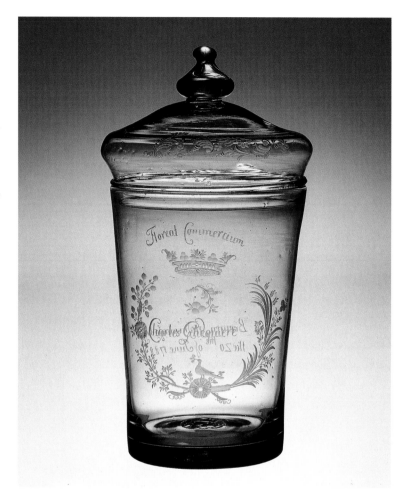

FIG. 5. XRF analysis of this signed and well-attributed John Frederick Amelung tumbler showed that Amelung used a unique formulation for making colorless glass objects. Such knowledge is useful when conservators and curators are attempting to authenticate glass objects claimed to be by Amelung.

ferences in the visual contrast of the radiograph. For example, the pigment lead white is a very strong absorber of X rays, producing a whitish or opaque region on the radiograph. Calcite, a calcium carbonate, contains calcium, which does not absorb X rays very well, thus producing a darker image on the radiograph. Other factors, such as thickness of the paint layers, also affect the absorption of X rays.

N. C. Wyeth's painting *Wyeth Family Mural* (1925) is a picture of the artist's family *(fig. 6)*. A radiograph of the painting, however, reveals an earlier painting executed in 1919 *(fig. 7)*. Wyeth apparently reused the canvas to create the composition that we now see. On the radiograph, the shirt of the man on the right was painted with lead white, producing a nearly opaque image on the X-ray film. The lighter shades of gray result from pigments containing lighter elements, executed in differing thicknesses. Without an X-ray image of the painting, we might never have known its true history.

DESTRUCTIVE (SAMPLING) ANALYSIS: Although nondestructive analysis can be used widely, in some cases, a sample is needed in order to gain the desired information. The identification of a surface coating, a paint-binding medium, or a pigment or corrosion product requires the removal of a small amount of material from the object. However, the sample removed is barely visible to the human eye. It is taken from a discrete area; the work of art is not disfigured, and its visual impact and value are not lessened.

Fourier Transform Infrared Microspectroscopy: A very important technique for the identification of artists' materials is Fourier transform infrared microspectroscopy

FIGS. 6, 7. These images show N. C. Wyeth's painting *Wyeth Family Mural* (1925) as it appears to viewers and a radiograph of the painting. The radiograph image shows an earlier painting executed in 1919 as an illustration for "Mildest Mannered Man," a short story published in the January 1919 issue of *Everybody's Magazine.*

(FTIR). For this process, a tiny sample is required—usually no larger than the head of a pin. The passage of infrared radiation through the sample results in a graph or spectrum that gives information on the chemistry of the various materials present (fig. 8). FTIR is particularly useful for classifying organic materials: the paint medium, the adhesive, or the surface coating of an object. Many inorganic materials also produce characteristic infrared spectra, so a single spectrum may result in information on both pigment and binding medium. With information gained from FTIR, for example, a conservator can choose the appropriate methods to remove an old, discolored surface coating.

Chromatography: Certain destructive techniques can be particularly useful for the positive identification of organic materials, such as binding media or coatings on a painting. Gas chromatography (GC) and high-pressure liquid chromatography (HPLC) can be used to separate complex mixtures of organic materials into their individual chemical components, providing a sort of chemical fingerprint. When

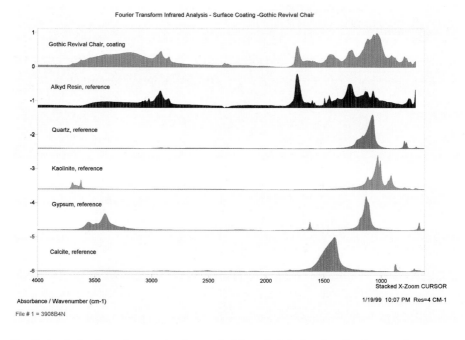

Fig. 8. Analysis of a surface coating from a Gothic-revival chair using Fourier transform infrared microspectroscopy (FTIR) reveals the presence of a modern alkyd resin and four inorganic materials (quartz, kaolinite clay, gypsum, and calcite). Knowing the makeup of the chair's surface coating can help a conservator decide how to safely remove the old coating.

coupled with mass spectrometry (MS), either technique permits the unequivocal identification of components in a particular material. GC-MS has been used quite successfully to identify the kind of drying oil (linseed, walnut, or poppy seed) used in western European paintings. This information may allow for the attribution of a particular work to a particular region or time period.

Keep in mind that it is not the responsibility of the scientist to condemn a work of art based solely on analytical data. Questions about an object's authenticity should be followed up with curatorial opinion. It is also wise to trace the object's provenance, or history of ownership. A combination of expert opinions backed by scientific fact is necessary in all authentication cases.

✑ *Working with a Professional*

Several museums in the United States house analytical laboratories (see Institutions with Analytical Facilities), and many of those will accept outside requests. However, not all museum laboratories can provide the same analytical services. It is important to discuss your particular problem with a museum scientist, who can help in the selection of proper technique(s) and advise on sampling. If the analytical instrumentation that is required is not available at your local museum, the scientist can suggest an appropriate alternative. Some university and hospital laboratories are experienced in the analysis of artistic and historic objects.

Commercial analytical laboratories with little experience with artworks are another alternative. However, although these professionals are experienced analysts, they may have had little exposure to artworks or artists' materials and thus may be unclear as to how to proceed or how to interpret the resulting data. In these instances, it is even more important that the collector discuss questions and the resulting data with a conservation science professional.

Curatorial and conservation approaches to the examination of artistic and historic objects can each provide significant information. Scientific analysis via the application of sophisticated instrumentation can give a third, and more objective, perspective to such examinations, providing new insights into the nature of materials used. All scientific analysis, however, has limitations. The knowledgeable collector recognizes that a combination of all three approaches is needed for the best understanding of an object.

Fig. 1. The preservation of the diverse objects that fall under the category *books, manuscripts, and ephemera* depends upon good storage and careful handling.

Books, Manuscripts, and Ephemera

LOIS OLCOTT PRICE

Old leather-bound books...overstuffed scrapbooks...creased and worn manuscripts...parchment deeds...travel-stained maps...family diaries...vintage postcards...paper dolls and other printed ephemera—all these items are paper-based *(fig. 1)*. As such, they share many of the same preservation concerns as artwork on paper, such as hand-colored prints or original drawings. But there is one major difference; these items must be handled directly and repeatedly if we are to retrieve the information and images they hold. Books must be opened, manuscript leaves turned, blueprints unrolled, and postcards flipped through. Fortunately, there are procedures designed to make these objects accessible while still preserving them.

Nature of the Materials

Structurally, books are the most complex objects in this group. They range from single-section pamphlets that are stapled or sewn through the spine to cloth-cased books with embossed covers and gold-tooled leather-bound books that are sewn on raised bands. The most common materials used include text papers, printers ink, decorative papers, various adhesives, leather, parchment, fabric, hemp cord, and thread. This mixed collection of materials that we call the book must be able to flex and provide support throughout the structure for the volume to function. Problems occur when one or more of the materials in a book becomes weak or rigid. Then the covers fall off, the pages loosen, and the paper tears and splits.

Manuscripts and documents are composed of paper or parchment leaves inscribed with printed and handwritten ink and are adorned with seals, ribbons, and postal stamps. They are often creased, torn, soiled from mailing and handling, and faded (if they have been displayed for a significant period of time). In addition, the iron-gall ink most commonly used from the eighth century through the opening decades of the twentieth century often weakens and corrodes the paper support. This highly acidic ink has a characteristic light brown to brown-black tone.

Printed ephemera such as postcards; trade, baseball, and greeting cards; paper dolls; theater programs; political brochures; and advertising fliers were never intended to survive—hence their designation as ephemera. They are printed on papers of widely varying quality in every conceivable type of ink and surface finish. At their initial distribution, they were commonly folded in half, shoved in a pocket, tacked on a wall, or wrapped around soap, chewing tobacco, or candy. If ephemera survived beyond its initial exposure, the next stop was often a scrapbook, trunk, or shoebox in a hot attic or damp basement.

Scrapbooks—blank books commonly filled with printed ephemera, newspaper clippings, and photographs—frequently are made with paper that is of poor quality and binding structures that are too weak or too rigid to support the contents. Adhesives used to attach the contents often weaken, discolor, and fail, leaving loose and detached photos, clippings, and theater programs floating through a deteriorating structure.

Maps, design drawings, and blueprints are often oversize and present special challenges. Maps vary from folded road maps to large wall maps mounted on muslin and rolled around a wooden bar. Design drawings document structures, transportation equipment, landscapes, and the work of decorative arts and industrial craftsmen. They can be executed in pencil, ink, and watercolor on paper, tracing paper, and drafting cloth. The term *blueprint* is a generic one for many different photoreproductive processes that vary widely in appearance and stability. In spite of their varied components, oversize materials share two defining characteristics that present special preservation problems: (1) their size makes safe handling and storage difficult; (2) their past function often involved heavy use and exposure to light and dirt.

ᔐ *What You Can Do*

Other than a poor environment, handling is the primary cause of deterioration for books, manuscripts, and ephemera. Even the gentle but repeated use of fragile materials will result in deterioration. Therefore, the first steps in a preservation program are the improvement of handling techniques and the use of protective enclosures.

The handling guidelines required by most libraries can be applied to private collections as well. Clean, dry hands are critically important. Since wearing gloves makes book leaves and individual manuscripts difficult to handle, they are seldom used. To avoid staining and attracting insects, never consume food in proximity to your valued collections. Only pencil should be used for taking notes. Avoid "sticky notes," which leave a damaging residue. Photocopying or scanning on a flatbed copier severely strains bound materials and often results in a damaged binding structure. Whenever possible, use book copiers that reproduce one page at a time while one half of the book is supported at a comfortable angle *(fig. 2)*. Many university and public libraries have these copiers.

Fig. 2. This photocopier is designed so the page to be copied rests on the glass while a shelf supports the rest of the text at a gentle angle. Copying done in this manner will not force the gutter of the text flat or strain the potentially weak and brittle spine, paper, sewing thread, or adhesive. Avoid flatbed copying, which causes much of the damage to bound materials.

Appropriate protective enclosures consist of boxes, sleeves, and folders designed to provide physical support. These will be made from stable, archival-quality papers, cardboards, bookcloths, and plastics that will not deteriorate with time and damage the objects that they enclose. Papers and cardboards must be acid-free and lignin-free. Acidity and lignin, a component of unpurified wood-pulp paper, cause paper to become weak, brittle, and discolored. Archival-quality papers and cardboards usually contain calcium carbonate, an alkaline salt that increases their protective capacity by absorbing acidity from the environment and the object. Stable plastics include uncoated polyester (such as Mylar D or Melinex 516), polypropylene, and polyethylene. Archival-quality papers should be inserted in plastic enclosures with objects whenever possible. The best way for you to obtain quality products is to purchase supplies from knowledgeable vendors who specialize in archival materials (see List of Suppliers).

Matting and framing provide a different type of protective enclosure for items that are intended for exhibit rather than storage. Unbound materials destined for exhibit require the same considerations as art on paper when choosing appropriate matting materials and techniques (see chapter 9, "Paper").

The shelving or drawers used to store your collection should also be composed of stable materials. The most readily available storage furniture is powder-coated or archival-quality baked enamel steel. These coating processes ensure that the storage furniture will not give off damaging solvent vapors, which can happen with wooden furniture, particularly in a closed environment such as a drawer or bookcase. If wooden furniture must be used, it should be coated with a stable, properly cured resin recommended by a conservation professional, or it should be lined with a layer of archival-quality paper and plastic. All closed spaces should be ventilated.

Heavily soiled materials must be cleaned before they can be safely handled or stored. Books in stable condition can be cleaned by holding them firmly closed while lightly vacuuming the edges of the text and outside covers with a brush attachment covered with cheesecloth. The outside of rolled blueprints or design drawings can be gently wiped with a soft, dry cloth. No attempt should be made to clean the image area of any object without consulting a conservation professional. If small amounts of dry, inactive mold residues are present, all cleaning must take place in a ventilated area. Avoid skin contact and minimize inhalation of dust and mold residue. If mold is active or present in quantity, consult a conservation professional.

℘ Books

As books age, their component materials become increasingly weak and inflexible. Proper support for the book structure whenever it is opened can help compensate for this deterioration. A book should never be forced beyond its natural opening, which can be as narrow as forty-five degrees in a book that has been bound too tightly. The covers should be supported by foam wedges or padded blocks *(fig. 3)*. Narrow "snake weights" can help to gently hold the book open. If a book is exhib-

Fig. 3. This large volume, like any book, requires adequate support whenever it is opened. Very few books can open flat on a table without the binding structure becoming strained. Foam, cardboard, and Plexiglas supports and cradles can be homemade or ordered from vendors listed in the List of Suppliers. Notice the weighted, fabric-covered "snake" that restrains the leaf at the corner. Demonstrated also is the proper method of turning pages, carefully from the top corner.

ited open for more than a day or two, it needs a cradle that is custom-designed to provide full support for the covers and spine.

Once a book is open and properly supported, pages should be turned from the top corner. Turning from the bottom edge can result in tears if the paper is weak. A thin card (rather than a moistened finger) inserted under the corner of the page can assist in turning pages. Never turn an open book upside-down. Use bookmarks of thin, good-quality paper rather than something thick, such as a pencil, which will strain the binding structure. Never use a book of value to press flowers or botanical specimens, which may stain the paper. Further, their moisture can cause mold growth. Prolonged contact with newspaper clippings and other poor-quality materials will also stain paper.

Proper shelving provides books with critically needed support (*fig. 4*). Average-size books should be shelved upright side-by-side so they lightly, but firmly, support one another. Bookends maintain books in an upright position and prevent the splaying, leaning, and sprawling that stress and damage the binding structure. Oversize books (those more than twelve inches in either direction) should be shelved separately. When shelved with average-size books, they are not adequately supported by adjacent volumes. Folio books (those more than fifteen inches in either direction) should be shelved flat and stacked no more than two to three high. In an upright position, the text blocks of these volumes are too heavy for adequate support by the binding structure. Oversize books in weak and deteriorated bindings should also be shelved flat.

When a book is removed from the shelf, careful handling will prevent damage to the binding. The books on either side should be pushed in slightly; then grasp the spine and remove the book from the shelf. Removal by the headcap at the top of the spine often tears and damages the binding.

Book boxes provide incomparable preservation benefits when a book is not in use. These protective enclosures prevent soiling and abrasion, act as a buffer against changes in relative humidity, and maintain the book structure in its most stable configuration when it is on the shelf or being transported. Book boxes vary from simple, four-flap enclosures made from folder-weight paper or cardboard to custom, clamshell boxes covered in book cloth (*fig. 5*). Some can be homemade while others can be ordered from vendors (see List of Suppliers). It is difficult to remove and reinsert books in slipcases without causing abrasion or other damage, so they are not recommended. Polyester film wrappers are available to protect dust jackets.

Fig. 4. The top shelf illustrates properly shelved books. Small books are separated from average-size volumes so that they will not become lost or damaged on the shelf. Wide bookends with rounded edges hold
books of similar size upright, ensuring adequate support. Large folios are shelved flat. The bottom shelf
illustrates several problems. There are no bookends, so the books lean and sprawl across the shelf, warping and straining their binding structures and allowing dust to collect inside the books. The text of the
large book *(left of center)* is falling out of its binding because it was shelved with the spine up. The spine
of the book at the far right was badly damaged when someone pulled it off the shelf incorrectly.

FIG. 5. Book boxes provide protection and structural support. The four-flap enclosure at the top left and the tuxedo box at the top right can hold small books and pamphlets. The phase box in the top center is appropriate for larger books, as are the rare-book and clamshell boxes in the foreground. The tuxedo box can be made with a few hand tools. The others are available from vendors listed in the List of Suppliers.

Books in poor condition also benefit from book boxes, which keep weak and detached pieces, such as covers and spines, together. If a box is unavailable, tie the book with flat cotton twill. If the leather is flaking and powdery, boxing helps prevent adjacent materials (and the reader) from getting soiled. The temptation to use leather dressings and oils should be resisted. This practice is no longer recommended for any leather binding; its past use frequently has resulted in leather deterioration and embrittlement (see chapter 4, "Organic Materials").

ᕬ   *Manuscripts and Documents*

As the paper in manuscripts ages, it may become increasingly discolored, weak, and brittle. The degree to which it deteriorates will depend upon its original manufacture and the environment in which it has lived. Paper may be weak and split along creases; seals may be cracked or partially detached; and acidic iron-gall ink may have weakened the text paper. For these reasons, manuscripts should be handled carefully by using a folder or separate sheet of archival-quality paper to support each leaf. If the paper is folded, it may be possible to gently open it; if it is too damaged or brittle to unfold safely, do not force it.

Parchment, also known as vellum, is a treated animal skin that generally remains quite strong. It is, however, reactive to changes in relative humidity, which cause it to cockle and distort. Parchment is not as flexible as paper and strongly resists unfolding. Do not force it. Relaxation and flattening of the skin will require the advice or assistance of a conservator. Like paper manuscripts, parchment may have cracked or partially detached seals. In addition, some parchment documents have flaking ink and should not be handled or flexed. In these instances, you should seek the immediate attention of a professional.

Archival-quality boxes and folders provide protective enclosures for manuscripts (*fig. 6*). Upright document boxes and folders are available in letter and legal sizes. Manuscripts should be placed in folders within these boxes; folders are then arranged so they provide firm but gentle support. Add a spacer if there are not enough folders to fill the box. Remove staples and paper clips whenever possible. Torn, brittle, or badly deteriorated manuscripts can be stabilized by placing them, individually, in polyester film folders that cling to the paper and provide good physical support. A sheet of archival-quality paper should be interleaved between manuscripts in paper folders and inserted in polyester folders behind single-sided material. Oversize, flat storage boxes and folders are available for larger objects.

Printed Ephemera

Printed ephemera must be handled and supported carefully. Protective enclosures of widely varying shapes and sizes best address the challenge. Archival vendors provide a good selection of boxes and protective plastic sleeves that are often sized to particular classes of ephemera. Individual archival-quality plastic sleeves are usually the best choice since they provide both good visibility and protection from handling. For additional support, you can cut lightweight archival-quality folder stock to the proper size and slip it into a plastic sleeve behind the object. Depending upon the condition and inherent fragility, most objects up to eight by ten inches can be

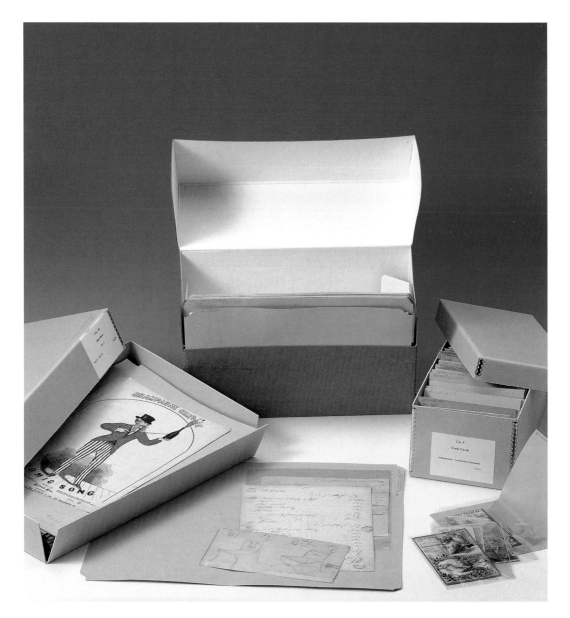

FIG. 6. Archival-quality boxes, folders, and clear plastic sleeves provide support and protection for manuscripts and printed ephemera. Letter-and legal-size documents, like those in the center, should be placed upright in folders that are stored in document boxes. To ensure adequate support, a spacer is necessary for partially filled boxes. Oversize material, such as the sheet music on the left, can be housed in individual folders placed in flat storage boxes. Small items, such as the trade cards on the right, can be put in individual plastic sleeves, grouped in folders, and then stored upright in archival "shoe" boxes.

housed upright in boxes once they have been placed in individual sleeves. Some plastic sleeves have multiple pockets and can be used in binders or albums. Larger objects should be housed flat in the same type of flat storage boxes that are used for larger manuscripts.

∾ Scrapbooks

Scrapbooks present some of the most difficult challenges in the preservation world. They require special care and consideration every time they are opened. The covers must be supported to avoid stress on the binding. The pages must be turned slowly, and support must be provided for loose or detached items. The original location of any detached items should be noted. Fragile items can be placed in labeled envelopes. The use of a book box that is strong and rigid enough to support and protect the scrapbook is imperative for any preservation effort. Ideally, all scrapbooks should be maintained intact. Sometimes, however, this is not possible. A conservation professional can help to make this determination and suggest alternatives.

∾ Oversize Materials

Oversize materials present special preservation challenges with respect to handling and storage. Appropriate protective enclosures to provide adequate support are critical to safe handling. Whenever the material is moved and used, there must be adequate space for the item so that it does not bump adjacent objects; safe handling may require two people. There are enclosures designed specifically to help you safely navigate your prized possessions down narrow halls, doorways, and corners.

Whenever possible, oversize materials should be stored flat. Maps and design drawings can be gently unfolded or unrolled if they are strong enough. They can be placed under a light weight (such as mat board with a book on each corner) and left for a few weeks to relax. A mildly humid environment is actually helpful. Take care that no splits or additional creases are formed. When leaving material partially folded, you should avoid cross-folds. If the material is brittle, torn, or resistant to flattening, seek the advice of a conservator.

Flat oversize material can be stored in oversize boxes or flat files. In either case, the objects should be placed in folders of heavy paper (.02-inch folder stock) or clear polyester film. An additional layer of rigid board adhered to the outside of the folder may be required to ensure safe handling. Heavy paper folders can hold up to five maps in good condition if they are interleaved with bond-weight archival-quality paper. Polyester film folders are appropriate for individual items that will be viewed frequently or are brittle, torn, or in weakened condition. The same interleaving paper should be inserted behind objects in polyester folders. However, polyester film cannot be used for drawings done in charcoal, pastel, or any loose media since such materials will offset onto the plastic.

When flat storage is impossible, rolled storage is the alternative. Many oversize maps and drawings have already been tightly rolled and may have suffered tears, creases, and distortion. If they are still reasonably flexible and severely torn, their condition can be improved by gently rolling them around a rigid tube that is four to six inches in diameter *(fig. 7)*. Archival-quality tubes can be purchased from numerous vendors (see List of Suppliers). If such tubes are unavailable, a carpet tube can be covered with layers of polyester film and archival-quality paper. The map or drawing should be rerolled in its original direction. Once rolled, cover the outside with a layer of archival-quality paper tied loosely with a flat cotton twill tape.

Photoreproductions of design drawings, generically called blueprints, present special problems because some are unstable and may cause damage to adjacent materials. Also, some are sensitive to the alkaline material used in many papers and storage enclosures. To avoid damage, photoreproductions should be stored separate from other collection materials. Follow the same procedures as those for maps and design drawings. The same boxes and folders can be used, but interleave objects with neutral, unbuffered papers that do not contain calcium carbonate.

ﻼ   *When to Call a Professional*

Through careful handling and the use of protective enclosures, an individual owner can take large and fundamental strides in preserving a collection. There are occasions, however, when a conservation professional is necessary to answer a complex question or treat a serious problem. The following situations require the advice of a conservation professional:

- Severe tears, particularly in oversize material, that cannot be stabilized with a polyester film folder require professional care. Pressure-sensitive tapes are not appropriate for use on any material of long-term value because they discolor and

Fig. 7. This large blueprint is being rolled around an archival tube, which is covered with an unbuffered paper that will not damage the image of this photoreproduction. Small weights restrain the free ends. Once rolled, the print will be covered with a piece of medium-weight paper and secured with twill ties, as is the roll in the background. Cardboard spacers at either end suspend the tube above the storage surface, preventing distortion of the rolled object.

damage paper as they age. While there are some tapes marketed as "archival," none are safe for all materials.

- Excessive or active mold can be a serious health hazard as well as damaging to collection material. Seek the help of a conservation professional for treatment.

- Severely brittle paper, particularly in a book or scrapbook, will require disbinding, customized support, or other specialized preservation measures.

- Rolled or folded paper that cannot gently and safely be opened should be left in the hands of a conservator.

- Books that exhibit broken sewing and loose or detached boards or leaves will require special care.

A conservation professional for books, manuscripts, and ephemera may be a paper conservator, a book conservator, a bookbinder with conservation experience, or a professionally trained technician or conservation assistant. Most will be members of the American Institute for Conservation (AIC) and/or the Guild of Bookworkers. These professional organizations provide opportunities for training and continuing education. A conservator or special-collections librarian at a state historical society or major research library may also be able to provide a sound recommendation.

ת

The foundation of any effort to preserve books, manuscripts, and ephemera lies in the use of protective enclosures and careful handling techniques. Most individuals, given good supplies and adequate information, can carry out such measures themselves. As simple as they seem, these steps will contribute profoundly to the long-term life of any collection.

C H A P T E R

4

Organic Materials

BRUNO P. POULIOT

*C*ollections of objects from around the world include a wide range of what can be termed *organic materials*: wood, leather, ivory, and feathers, to name a few. These materials are readily available from nature and have been used by humans since the beginning of time. Even though organic materials are most often associated with anthropology and natural history museums, they are also present in everyday objects and in art collections.

As a group, *organic materials* can best be defined as those products originating from once-living tissues, either from the plant or animal kingdom. The one characteristic that these materials share is that they are porous to varying degrees. Since they come from living tissues, pores are essential to allow nutrients to pass through for growth and sustenance. This characteristic of organic materials is important because it means that they continually absorb or lose moisture, depending on the conditions of the surrounding air. Along with moisture, they also absorb other compounds carried in the air, such as dirt, airborne chemicals, and pollutants, which in turn affect their long-term stability. In other words, these materials are quite sensitive to their environment and will therefore last much longer if cared for properly.

The good news is that there is much you can do to ensure that the organic materials found in your home or in your collection will be preserved in good condition for as long as possible. In order to understand how these materials will respond over time and what you can do to preserve them, they are best divided into four main groups.

✺   *Plant Materials*

The first group of organic materials consists of plant materials: wood, bark, leaves, and any other parts of a plant or tree. These are all composed mainly of cellulose, a long molecule related to common sugar. Almost all basketry items are made of plant materials. The same is true for most furniture, many types of carvings, masks, and numerous utilitarian objects (see chapter 11, "Furniture," for joined wooden objects).

Plant materials may have been used in their raw state, or they may have been processed before use—for instance, by soaking in water or other substances to remove unwanted by-products or to extract fibers. The surfaces of these materials may also have been enhanced by the addition of dyes, colors, finishes, or paints. Any of these procedures or additions to the original plant material will affect the way it behaves over time, sometimes improving its longevity but more often accelerating its decay.

Generally, plant materials will last longer in a dry, cool environment. They will also benefit from relatively low light levels and from being kept away from the ultraviolet radiation that is present in sunlight and many types of fluorescent lighting. In fact, in addition to causing bleaching of the plant materials themselves, fading of the paints and dyes, and yellowing of the surface finishes, excessive light will also cause an increased acidity that results in a more brittle and weak material. When items made of plant material begin to shed excessively or when fine cracks become visible all over the surface, a likely culprit is excessive acidity, which is exacerbated by too much light.

Another important characteristic of plant materials is their relative flexibility. Most were quite pliable when their tissues were still alive or just after they were harvested. This is the very reason they were chosen—for instance, to allow for the easy forming of a doll or weaving of a basket. Although plant materials that are formed into objects are now dry, they remain flexible to varying degrees; they will almost inevitably sag or lose their shape over time unless properly supported (*figs. 1, 2*). Hanging a basket by its handle is not recommended, as the handle is not built for constantly carrying weight over a prolonged period of time. Baskets should be displayed on shelves, where their weight will rest on the base, which in most cases is the strongest part of the construction.

Objects made of plant materials will also be susceptible to mold and to damage by insects and animal pests (silverfish, cockroaches, mice) that feed on the cellulosic components. These pests generally are unable to digest the cellulose unless the object is damp or impregnated with dirt and oils. If you keep objects that are made of plant materials dry and clean, you will diminish the likelihood of the problem ever developing in the first place.

Regular dusting with a soft brush may be all that is required for well-supported objects in relatively good condition to remain that way for years to come. Further cleaning, such as with water, should be left to a professional, as it may cause discoloration, staining, or alteration to the shape. Small breaks can probably be fixed at home with a few drops of a water-based adhesive, such as methyl cellulose or wheat starch, but any other major damage should be brought to the attention of a professional conservator.

Skins and Leathers

The second group of organic materials includes any type of skins, hides, leathers, furs, and related materials. Objects in this category are made from the skin or internal soft tissues of animals; the basic element of skins and leathers is collagen, a strong and fibrous protein. These materials are often quite strong and can be made flexible through processes such as tanning, which explains their wide usage by humans since time immemorial.

Although skins and hides are sometimes used as raw materials, as in rawhide and sinew (tendons processed for use as cord or thread), they are most often processed in one form or another. Tanning stops decay and makes skins and hides more or less permanently supple. Such processing will, however, have a major impact on how these materials behave over time. For instance, leather manufactured in the nineteenth century was often vegetable-tanned—that is, prepared with tannin extracted from plants or trees. Some vegetable-tanned leathers have been found to be especially sensitive to a form of degradation called *red rot*, which occurs when

Figs. 1, 2. This nineteenth-century corn-husk doll is a good example of an object made from plant material. Such dolls were a Native American tradition copied by early American settlers and are still produced today in some areas of the United States. This doll is displayed on a felt-padded custom-made brass support. Such a stand is recommended as it unobtrusively supports the weight of the object without putting undue stress on any part of the doll. Thumb tacks, often used in the past to display such items, cause irreversible tears, holes, and stains on organic materials and should be avoided.

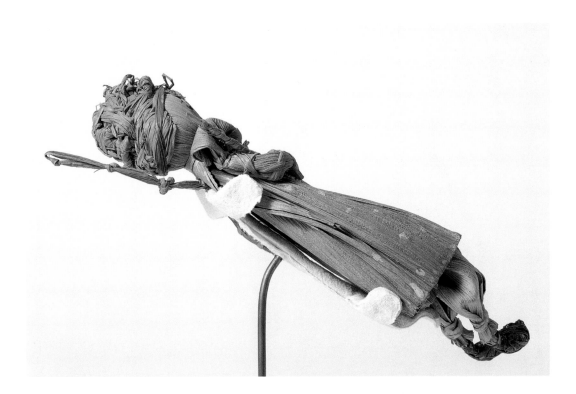

the leather is exposed to excessive acidity, either through the tanning process or through contact with pollutants in the air *(figs. 3, 4)*.

Almost all types of skin-based products will remain permanently sensitive to the effects of water, which washes away some of the tanning components, causes irreversible stains, and leaves the material more vulnerable to degradation. Besides being kept dry, all types of skins and leathers benefit tremendously if kept in a cool, moderately lit environment. Heat actually increases the rate of decay and enhances desiccation, or drying, of the skins. Excessive light will cause fading and degradation of the oils and lubricants that are present.

Because of their collagen content, skin-based products are a food source for commonly found insects such as clothes moths and various types of beetles. You can help prevent infestation by keeping such materials clean and dry. If you discover active damage by insects, isolate the object by placing it in a sealed bag and immediately contact a professional conservator, who can recommend eradication measures. You should also call a professional pest control service that can deal with the more general problem of infestation in the location where the object was kept.

FIGS. 3, 4. This fire bucket is painted with the date "1776" and the name "Z. Titcomb." Fire buckets were common in early America, when each member of a fire company was required to provide his own. The handle shown on the bucket is a modern replacement; the leather on the original *(opposite)* became red, powdery, and weak (hence the term *red rot*) and broke off in several fragments. No completely satisfactory method exists yet to counteract this progressive degradation of leather, although a professional conservator will be able to consolidate what remains of the leather and suggest preventive measures to slow down the degradation process.

There is a common misconception that in order to remain beautiful and supple, leathers should be "dressed." In fact, dressing with oils or waxes, while a good preventive measure for leather that is being used regularly, has been found to be unnecessary and even harmful to leather objects in collections. This is because most of the common dressings change the natural acidity of leathers, reducing their longevity. Excessive use of dressing may also cause "spews," a waxy, white film that is hard to remove and is always disfiguring. As a rule, if they are in good condition, it is best to leave skins and leathers as they are. When they are very distorted, dry, or otherwise damaged, consult a professional conservator, who can assess the condition and use stable materials for their repair and long-term preservation.

℘ Ivory, Bone, and Shell

The third group among organic materials consists of ivory, bone, shell, and similar substances. They form the skeletal systems of animals and invertebrates and are composed of organic matters mixed with calcium salts. Although they share some similarities in chemical composition, all these materials grow in different

ways, which affects their behavior over time. Like other organic materials, ivory, bone, and shell have been used extensively for carvings, as decorative elements, and in utilitarian objects.

True ivory comes only from the teeth, or modified incisors (tusks), of various animals; bones come from the skeletal system. All teeth, and therefore ivories, are composed of a few closely associated layers with different characteristics. Bones, however, have the same composition throughout and are more porous, allowing for the passage of blood vessels. Both materials will react to changes in the environment by absorbing or releasing moisture. This causes shrinkage and expansion, which very often leads to cracks; ivory is particularly susceptible because of its multilayered structure *(fig. 5)*.

It is therefore important to keep objects made of ivory, bone, and shell in a relatively stable environment that is neither too wet nor too dry (35 percent to 55 percent relative humidity is best). You may want to display them in a case, where fluctuations in relative humidity and temperature will be minimal. However, heat can also be a problem, and no ivory or bone should be displayed in internally lit cases unless provisions have been made to avoid heat buildup within the case. For objects in storage, it is recommended to keep them wrapped or boxed in stable, nonacidic materials (see List of Suppliers). If cleaning is required, a cotton swab dampened in a solution consisting of a few drops of a mild detergent and a quart of clean water can be used, but it is crucial that these materials never become completely soaked. In fact, the careless use of water will cause dirt to become embedded in the pores and cracks, making it more visible than before. It is recommended that you consult a professional conservator when treatment beyond surface cleaning is required.

Light can also be detrimental to ivory, bone, and shell, bleaching these materials and causing a yellowing of the oils and waxes often used to bring out their

FIG. 5. *(opposite page)* The ivory seal *(right)* and bone dice cup *(left)* both date from the nineteenth century and demonstrate the type of damage often encountered with these materials. The ivory seal handle has cracked lengthwise as the ivory contracted over a rigid metallic core when the environment was too dry. Cracking often occurs when ivory is combined with materials that prevent its movement during fluctuations in relative humidity. A fair amount of dirt is now embedded in the crack, making it quite visible. A crack through bone, like the one visible in the dice cup, is less common. Cracking did occur here, however, because the wall of the cup is thin and was prevented from contracting due to the bottom piece, which is also made of bone.

luster. Air pollutants such as sulfur dioxide from car exhaust fumes and volatile acids released by some woods and other products can cause severe damage to objects made of shell. If you find that shells in your collection are becoming powdery or have developed crystals on their surface, you should contact a professional conservator. A conservator can identify the damaging factor and recommend the necessary protective measures.

⌁   *Horn, Tortoiseshell, and Feathers*

The fourth and last group of organic materials includes horn, feathers, tortoiseshell, hair, and similar materials that are outgrowths of the bodies of higher vertebrates and birds. All are basically composed of keratin, a sturdy type of protein. They have been used extensively over the years, either alone or in combination with other materials as decorative features (tortoiseshell inlays) or structural elements (corset stays made of whalebone).

The unique characteristics that these materials share are their malleability when subjected to high heat and moisture and the fact that they retain almost any form if allowed to cool in this new shape. Large ladles made of one piece of horn are created in this manner, as are large pieces of flat tortoiseshell used as veneers and inlays for furniture.

Although they are made of a rather resistant protein, these materials remain sensitive to fluctuations in relative humidity. They are porous and will contract and expand with changing environmental conditions, causing particular problems for those pieces that are thin or restrained by another material (*figs. 6, 7*).

Another characteristic of materials made of keratin is their general sensitivity to light. In fact, most are pigmented, and the colors, especially those found in feathers, are extremely light-sensitive. Unfortunately, there is nothing that can be done to restore the original colors once they have faded. Excessive light will also cause discoloration of the natural and applied oils within these materials, which will make objects appear more yellow and less translucent. Since they are made of proteins, they are also susceptible to damage by mold and pests. Regular inspection to check for the presence of insect carcasses, powdery deposits, or pin-size holes on the surface is essential to prevent an infestation from spreading and severely damaging your collection.

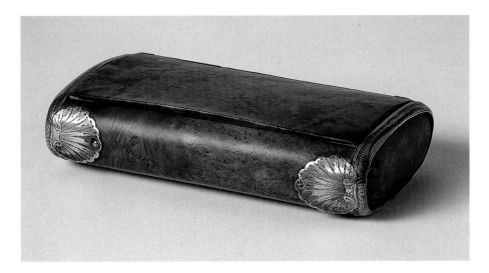

FIGS. 6, 7. This walnut burl box with tortoiseshell lining dates from the first half of the eighteenth century. The exquisite craftsmanship is still evident, but the tortoiseshell has warped extensively and has become partly detached from the wooden underlayer. This type of problem is sometimes impossible to treat without causing further damage. The application of heat to soften and realign the shell is not recommended, as it would cause damage to both the tortoiseshell and the wood.

ૢ

Either alone or in combination with other materials, organic materials will remain permanently sensitive to the environment in which they are kept, whether on display or in storage. There is much you can do (or not do) to ensure that these objects remain in good condition for your own enjoyment and that of future generations. Because organic materials are often combined with other materials *(fig. 8)*, there is no simple rule of thumb for their protection. However, a relatively stable, cool, low-light, and clean environment will do much to keep organic materials in good condition for a long time. Again, when faced with a severe or uncontrolled form of degradation or damage, consult a professional conservator.

FIG. 8. The battledore and shuttlecocks illustrated here demonstrate the varied use of organic materials. These items probably date from the middle of the nineteenth century and predate the creation of the official rules of the sport that we now call *badminton*. The battledore has a wooden frame with an embossed, gilded-leather covering and parchment stretched over the paddle to serve as a bouncing surface. The shuttlecocks are made of feathers stuck into cork that is covered with a silk velvet and a soft, white leather. Although they remain in good condition, these materials have become more fragile with age. They can, however, be enjoyed by generations to come if they are properly cared for now.

CHAPTER

5

Ceramics and Glass

MARGARET A. LITTLE

$\mathcal{C}$eramic and glass objects are part of our everyday lives; we eat from them, drink from them, cook in them, build with them, and view the world through them. Ceramic and glass objects are no longer simply thought of as functional; they are also valued as art objects that are created to be displayed, not used. Whether functional or decorative, the factors that determine the care and preservation of ceramic and glass objects are the same, as are the methods used in the preservation process.

Nature of the Materials and Fabrication

At first, the pairing of ceramic and glass objects in a discussion of collection care may seem illogical because on the surface the two materials appear to be so different. Glass objects are transparent or translucent and fragile; ceramic objects are generally opaque and, although breakable, have a greater appearance or feel of solidity. In fact, both are made of materials that are more similar than dissimilar—oxygen-rich compounds, mostly silicates, whose physical and chemical properties are defined (on a microscopic level) by the nature of the bond between silica and oxygen. Glass and ceramic objects vary in the source of the silica used to make them (usually quartz for glass and clay for ceramics) and in the additives that give the unique properties to the materials, such as the color of glass or the working properties of ceramics.

57

Ceramic objects are made from clay or claylike materials that, when wet, are pliable and can be transformed into a variety of shapes by hand, on a wheel, or in a mold. A single ceramic object can be made using a variety of techniques. After an object has been formed, it is air-dried and then fired in a kiln to remove any remaining water. At this point the clay becomes rocklike.

Clay bodies of ceramic objects can be divided into three categories—earthenware, stoneware, and porcelain—depending on the type of clay, additives, and firing temperature. The higher the firing temperature, the greater the fusion of clay particles and the less porous the ceramic will be. Earthenware is fired in the lowest temperature range and is more porous than stoneware, which is fired at the middle of the temperature range and is semiporous. Porcelain is fired in the highest temperature range; the clay particles become glasslike, and the ceramic is nonporous. The color of the different types of ceramic can vary. Earthenwares can be red, orange, brown, or white; stoneware can be white, gray, or brown; porcelain is always white.

The surface of a ceramic object can be finished in a number of ways. Before being fired in a kiln, the clay can be burnished to give it a smooth, glossy appearance, or designs can be stamped or incised into the surface. Other decorative techniques involve the application of slip (a fluid suspension of clay particles in water) or glaze (a glasslike coating) to the surface, either before or after the first kiln firing. Slips and glazes can be further embellished by the application of paint, enamel, or gold. For the most part, these types of decoration, which have been fired in a kiln, are stable but are susceptible to abrasion.

Glass is composed of four categories of materials: silica, which acts as a framework; fluxes, which lower the melting point of the silica; stabilizers, which ensure that the glass is not water soluble; and modifiers, which give glass specific properties. These materials and coloring agents are melted in a furnace. Glass objects are then formed by taking some of this molten mixture and blowing shapes freehand, blowing or forming it in a mold, or manipulating it into a shape with tools. Once a glassmaker has formed an object, it must be placed in a kiln to relieve the stress that builds up in the glass as it is worked. After it is removed from the kiln, the object is ready for further decoration. Designs can be engraved on the surface using a metal or abrasive engraving wheel or can be etched using an acid. Enamels, stains, paint, or gold can also be used to decorate the surface. This last category of decoration, essentially material applied to the surface of the glass, is susceptible to damage through abrasion.

℘ Deterioration

The deterioration of ceramic and glass objects can be divided into two categories: physical and chemical. Physical deterioration involves damage to the surface or body of the object and can range from abrasions or loss of the surface and decoration to cracks in the body to fragmentation *(fig. 1)*. These kinds of damage can result from the everyday use of an object or from poor handling. Ceramic and glass objects are prone to physical damage because their bodies, although hard, are brittle and therefore vulnerable if not handled carefully. Sometimes improper storage, such as stacking objects on top of one another, can cause cracking or breakage. Such damage can also be the result of ceramic and glass objects being subjected to extremes of temperature.

Fig. 1. Because the material from which ceramic and glass objects are made is hard and unyielding, these objects are particularly vulnerable to physical damage, such as cracks and breakage. In ceramics, cracks are often difficult to see, but their presence undermines the stability of the object. This earthenware plate broke when another object bumped against the rim. A crack already existed in the rim, and the pressure of the other object striking against it caused a section of the rim to break away.

Inherent vice—the intrinsic instability of the fabric of an object—can lead to physical deterioration. This kind of damage is difficult to prevent. When unrelieved stress builds up in the material during the fabrication process, even a slight bump on the edge or surface of an object can cause damage. When the glaze is not adequately attached to the ceramic body, it can easily be detached by slight pressure. When the glaze and the ceramic body expand and contract in different ways, a fine network of cracks (sometimes called *crazing*) will develop in the glaze. All these situations are examples of inherent vice leading to physical deterioration.

Physical damage can also occur to ceramic and glass objects because of previous restorations *(fig. 2)*. The field of ceramic and glass restoration/conservation has changed a great deal in the last one hundred years. It once was common to reassem-

FIG. 2. Restoration practices used in the past sometimes cause additional damage to an object. One common practice was the use of metal rivets or staples to reassemble ceramic and glass objects. Holes were drilled on either side of a break line, and a metal rivet was inserted into the holes. Fragments were held together by tension. The sweetmeat dish shown here underwent this type of repair, and numerous rivets were used. Sometimes, restorers made an effort to hide the rivets by drilling a channel in the surface between the holes and placing the rivet below the surface of the ceramic. The channels and holes were then filled and painted to blend with the surrounding ceramic body.

ble broken ceramic and glass objects using metal staples or rivets, to grind away broken edges that did not fit together, or to smooth chipped rims by abrading the roughness. These techniques have caused significant damage and are not employed today.

The chemical deterioration of ceramic and glass objects occurs when materials from which the object is made begin to break down due to their own instability (inherent vice) or to exposure to adverse external conditions. It is often a combination of these factors that leads to chemical deterioration, which, if unchecked, can result in the total *physical* deterioration of the object. In glass, an example of chemical deterioration that is the result of both inherent and external factors is a condition sometimes called *sick glass*. This occurs when there is an imbalance in the ingredients of the glass mixture. Depending on the nature of the imbalance, a layer of moisture can form on the glass surface, creating a slippery or soapy layer. Glass in this state will be described as "weeping." Glass made from an unbalanced glass mixture could also "crizzle." In this case, a fine network of cracks appears on the surface of the glass *(fig. 3)*. These reactions are frequently caused or accelerated by poor environmental conditions, such as high temperatures or high relative humidity.

In ceramics, a common type of chemical deterioration involves soluble salts in the clay body. Soluble salts can be present as a naturally occurring part of the clay from which the object is made, or they can enter the clay body from the environment, as in the case of archaeological ceramics, which acquire salts from the soil in which they are buried. Nonarchaeological objects can acquire soluble salts in the course of normal use—for example, if the ceramic is used to store a material containing salt. Soluble salts respond to changes in relative humidity, becoming soluble in high humidity and crystallizing in low humidity. This cycle causes physical damage to the ceramic body and surface decoration because the salt crystals are larger than liquid salt. The first indication that there are soluble salts in a ceramic may be the appearance of a white haze on the surface, which is actually the salt crystallizing. Eventually, the decorative surface of the ceramic or the ceramic object itself begins to crumble; eventually the object could be reduced to a pile of dust.

Other kinds of chemical deterioration include staining of ceramics—usually caused by contact with water-based substances that penetrate the porous body of the object and create a color change—and etching of glass or glaze surfaces by acidic materials. It is sometimes possible to remove stains from ceramics, but etched surfaces cannot be repaired.

FIG. 3. The proportions of the four categories of materials used to make glass—silica, flux, stabilizer, and modifiers—must be in balance for a glass item to be stable. If they are not, conditions such as "weeping" or "crizzling" may occur. In this broken glass, a fine network of cracks has appeared on the surface, which will eventually spread throughout the glass. Crizzled surfaces are fragile, and small fragments of glass can easily be lost. High temperatures or relative humidity can catalyze weeping and crizzling in glass, or accelerate the process.

৯   What You Can Do

Collectors frequently ask how they can best preserve their ceramic and glass collections and what kinds of preservation tasks they can undertake on their own. In answer to the first question, preventing physical damage to ceramic and glass objects is the easiest and most important step in their preservation. It is always better to prevent damage from occurring than to undertake an expensive conservation or restoration treatment after the fact. When handling an object, it is important to use both hands and to be sure that your grasp is secure. Never pick up a ceramic or glass object by the handle alone or by the finial of a cover; these areas tend to be weak and break easily.

Cotton or latex gloves are sometimes recommended for handling collectible objects to protect surfaces from the harmful effects of oils found on skin. Skin oils have a negligible effect on ceramic and glass objects, but wearing gloves certainly will help keep the surfaces clean. But because ceramic and glass items have smooth surfaces, gloves may not provide the wearer a good "grip," and an object could slip and break. You should use your own judgment when deciding whether to wear gloves.

As mentioned earlier, ceramic and glass objects can be both functional and decorative. When objects are used, they are at great risk for physical damage. You need to decide whether your ceramic and glass objects are for everyday use or merely for display. For instance, should an heirloom set of Wedgwood china be used at holiday dinners or remain in a cabinet? Although wear and tear on such objects (abrasion of the decorative surfaces, the increased risk of staining or breakage) is great, a collector may decide that tradition outweighs the needs of preservation, or vice versa. Whatever the decision, the choice should be an informed one.

Correct display and storage play an important part in long-term preservation. For example, you may want to line storage shelves with a thin layer of ethafoam (polyethylene foam) or bubble wrap, which provides a nonskid, cushioned surface for the objects. If ceramic and glass items are stored in drawers, padding between them is recommended to prevent physical damage. If objects must be stacked or nested together in storage, make sure that lighter ones are placed on the top of the stack and that a cushioning material—a flannel cloth, ethafoam, or bubble wrap—is layered between the objects to prevent abrasion. Generally, inert materials are recommended for the storage of collections. These are materials that are nonacidic and do not adversely interact with an object and give off harmful chemicals or vapors as they disintegrate. For instance, uncoated wood used in shelving can give off acidic vapors as it ages and is not recommended for the storage of sensitive materials. While ceramics and glass can tolerate a wider range of environments than more sensitive materials, such as metals, use of inert materials for storage of ceramic and glass objects remains a wise preservation effort.

Ceramic and glass objects are not generally sensitive to elevated light levels, but as mentioned previously, some forms of chemical and physical deterioration can be catalyzed by extremes or fluctuations in temperature and relative humidity. Therefore, a stable temperature of 68°F (plus or minus three degrees) and a relative humidity of 50 percent (plus or minus 5 percent) should be maintained. Thus, you should choose display and storage areas carefully. In selecting optimum locations, avoid windows with unrestricted sunlight (which can cause temperature fluctuations), heaters or fireplaces, and exterior walls.

If a mount or case is needed for the display of an object, inert materials should be used. Display mounts made of Plexiglas, metal, and painted wood are commercially available and may be suitable. The most important caution in choosing a mount or display device is that it "fit" the object. That is, the mount should not exert pressure on the object but rather gently hold it in place. Many objects are damaged by display devices that are too tight and grind away the edge(s) of the object or cause breakage *(fig. 4)*.

Over time, most ceramic and glass objects will acquire a covering of dirt and grime on their surfaces. It may be possible to remove dirt by using a soft brush. If the decoration on the object is not loose or flaking and there do not appear to be any other physical problems, you can clean the surface with a lightly dampened cot-

FIG. 4. If an object requires a mount for display, care must be taken to ensure that the mount will safely hold the object without being too loose or too tight. The mount on this redware dish is too tight. At the top edge of the dish, the bare metal wire is visible. It is possible that the tightness of the wire caused some of the loss (chipped areas) seen at the top edge. Presently, the wire is grinding against the ceramic, causing further damage. An appropriate mounting system will securely hold an object in place without placing undue stress on it. It will also have padding of some kind (felt strips are often used) to prevent the mounting system from abrading the object.

ton flannel cloth. Water alone or a solution of water and a few drops of a mild dish-washing detergent can be used. Before any cleaning is attempted, examine the object closely to determine if there have been previous repairs that could be damaged by cleaning. Sometimes repairs are so convincing that they are not seen until they begin to disintegrate in cleaning *(figs. 5, 6)*.

੨ *When to Call a Professional*

When a ceramic or glass object requires more than simple surface cleaning or if you notice or are concerned about a change occurring in the object, you should contact a professional conservator.

FIGS. 5, 6. Often, repairs to ceramic objects are invisible in normal light. Such is the case with this ceramic tureen. In normal light, the repairs made to the neck, ear, torso, and foot are not visible *(left)*. However, when the object is viewed in ultraviolet light, the repairs fluoresce and become visible *(right)*. It is important to know when an object has been restored since the type of restoration may affect how the object is treated or maintained.

Because the field of object conservation is so broad (encompassing a wide variety of materials and problems), some objects conservators specialize and work only on ceramic and/or glass objects or with decorative arts or archaeological objects in particular. Once you have contacted a conservator, establish a dialogue. Be sure to outline your expectations for the treatment, and ask questions about the course of action recommended. A conservator may be able to address any questions or concerns you have about storage or display of the object or may suggest other professionals for you to contact. The conservator's examination of the object, treatment proposal, and the actual treatment should be documented with written reports and photographs.

In their treatment of ceramic and glass objects, conservators will strive to use techniques that are reversible and materials with good aging properties, ensuring that treatments do no additional damage. An important point to remember is that it will not be possible to use a ceramic or glass object after it has been treated. Although the treatments performed can hold up under most display situations, they cannot withstand the wear and tear of daily use.

To ensure the preservation of your ceramics and glass collections, there are a number of steps you should take. These include creating a safe storage and display environment, one that will not cause further deterioration of the objects; establishing safe handling procedures; understanding what kinds of preservation activities you can safely carry out on your own; and, most important, understanding when it is necessary to contact a professional conservator.

CHAPTER

Textiles

LINDA EATON

$\mathcal{W}$hat do pin cushions, oriental rugs, samplers, and designer dresses have in common? They are all made from textile fibers. Textiles can vary from the most mundane, homespun towel to the richest and most expensive silks and velvets. Textiles also can be simply one component of a composite object, such as upholstery on furniture. As numerous as the forms textiles can take are our reasons for wanting to properly care for them. Perhaps they are rare historic survivals or family heirlooms. Or perhaps they hold sentimental value, such as wedding dresses and christening gowns. Or we may simply want to ensure their survival for future generations. Some common questions about the care and preservation of textiles include:

How should I mount an heirloom sampler for framing? How can I safely display the quilt made by my great-grandmother? What can I do to protect my oriental rugs from insects? How can I clean the christening gown that has been passed down through generations?

The care and treatment of textiles varies with their size and shape and the materials from which they are made. Historically, textile products have been made from natural fibers, which are either proteins (wool and silk) or cellulosics (cotton, linen, hemp). More recent materials include modified natural fibers, such as rayon (first developed in the 1880s—earlier than most people think), and synthetics, such as nylon and polyester. Each fiber has different physical and chemical characteristics, which has implications for treatment and care. Textiles are created through a variety of techniques, including knotting, braiding, knitting, or weaving on a loom. They may be decorated with embroidery, or patterns may be applied with dyes or pigments. Other characteristics may be the result of a finishing technique; for example, early chintzes were often glazed with a starch or sugar coating to make them shiny. Many textile products also contain other materials. A seventeenth-century embroidery may include metal threads and mica, and historic clothing may have ivory buttons and steel "boning" to shape the bodice. All these materials need to be considered. However, some basic tenets of preservation are common to all textiles. The following are problems you may encounter and suggestions for how best to deal with them.

℘ Light

It is commonly known that light causes dyes to fade, but what is less well known is that the fibers themselves are physically damaged by light. Silk is particularly vulnerable as it is damaged not only by the invisible ultraviolet (UV) component of sunlight and most fluorescent lighting but also by light within the visible spectrum. Dyes are also faded by visible light *(fig. 1)*. Many people think that by filtering out the highly damaging UV light they have sufficiently protected their textiles, but this is not true. It helps, but only total darkness is completely safe.

The best way to prevent light damage to textiles is to keep them in the dark. Sound advice but not very practical if you want to display and enjoy them. There are, however, a number of ways that you can limit light damage. Most important, textiles should never be displayed in direct sunlight or even in bright reflected light. Museums keep light levels low (5 footcandles/50 lux) to preserve their collections; you can take the same measures in your home wherever the preservation of textiles is a concern. Because light damage is cumulative, another way to protect vulnerable objects is to limit the time they are exposed. Consider displaying them for just part of the year (keeping them in proper storage for the remainder) or displaying them with a curtain or cover of some sort that can be drawn aside when necessary.

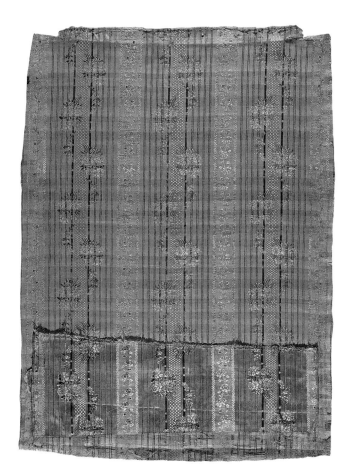

FIG. 1. These two pieces of fabric once had the same brilliant colors. The larger piece was used as upholstery on a chair for approximately twenty years. The smaller fragment was excess material that was cut from the larger piece and kept in a box in dark storage. Exposure to visible light not only caused a complete loss of color but also resulted in structural damage to silk fibers, making them very brittle. This physical damage is evident along the top edge of the fabric.

๑ Mold and Mildew

Mold and mildew cause irreversible damage, but prevention is fairly easy: do not keep historic textiles in bags or boxes in attics or damp basements. Store them in the part of the house where you control the climate for your own personal comfort. Wrapping and padding textiles with materials such as acid-free tissue or clean cotton sheets, which can themselves absorb moisture, will reduce the risk of mold or mildew damage. If the damage is limited to a musty smell, airing the piece will eventually help. For active mold growth, pieces should be unwrapped and aired until dry. The mold then can be carefully removed using a vacuum with a HEPA (High Efficiency Particulate Air) filter. Many domestic vacuum cleaners now include these filters. Unfortunately, most staining and discoloration is irreversible.

℘ Insects

Wool is vulnerable to attack by moths and carpet beetles. Starched cottons and linens may be attacked by silverfish. Good housekeeping is key; this should involve periodic inspection and careful surface cleaning before storage. Museums avoid the use of insecticides and mothballs, which can pose a health and safety risk. Research has shown that cedar closets are ineffective in themselves. In most cases, it is probably the higher level of basic care and handling associated with this type of storage that prevents infestations. Major infestations should be dealt with by professionals.

If individual pieces are attacked, they should be isolated immediately in a plastic bag—or plastic sheeting for larger pieces—and sealed with tape. Once the textile is sealed in a bag, it can be put in a freezer. Freezing is a technique used extensively by museums. A domestic freezer will do if it is not overfilled. The rapid lowering of temperature to around -20°F is the key. Freeze the object for three days, slowly bring it back up to room temperature, and then freeze it for another three days. The whole textile should then be carefully vacuumed to remove dead insects and residue. Freezing can cause damage to other types of materials often associated with textiles, so when in doubt, seek professional advice.

℘ Inherent Vice

Sometimes damage is caused by the very nature of the textiles themselves, referred to by professionals as inherent vice. Often there is little that can be done about it. Inherent vice includes the rapid deterioration found in weighted silk (silk that has been treated with metallic salts or tannins to literally increase its weight) or dark colors, such as many blacks and browns (the iron salts often used in the dyeing process accelerate the degradation process). A few rare dyes will even fade in the dark. Good preventive care and storage can slow the inevitable degradation process.

➢ *Cleaning*

Most people have experience with washing some kinds of textiles. We all have to clean our own clothes and household linens. But cleaning historic textiles is different. Conservators hesitate to clean them too often. (Just think how much damage is done to T-shirts by repeated washing in a machine.) Each cleaning process causes a little damage; with historic textiles you need to weigh the benefit against the risk to the object.

➢ *Surface Cleaning*

When surface dirt is the problem, careful vacuuming can make a significant difference to the appearance of a textile *(fig. 2)*. Low suction power should be used. Vacuuming through screening can prevent individual yarns and fibers from being pulled and lost. It is amazing what a difference careful surface cleaning can make. Frequently, this is the only type of cleaning that is necessary, and it is often the only type of cleaning that is possible without damaging the textile.

➢ *Washing*

The fibers in historic textiles are usually already weakened and brittle, and they become even more vulnerable when wet. Dyes can bleed. Textiles and seams may shrink, and stitching may pucker. Finishes may be lost. Degraded textiles may not be flexible enough to reblock into shape without splitting. Stains that have been in place for some time are often impossible to remove. Ironically, cleaning the whole textile can actually make the stains look worse. Harsh bleaching can result in a hole rather than a stain; even mild bleaches cause damage to the polymer chains that make up fibers. Conservators are not being secretive when they hesitate to give advice on cleaning. Cleaning is an irreversible process. Once the damage is done, there is often nothing that can be done to remedy the situation *(fig. 3)*. If you have any doubts, it is always best to consult a professional.

Textile conservators working within museums take an academic approach to cleaning, avoiding commercial detergents, which usually contain unwanted components, such as brighteners or enzymes. Sometimes they instead use other chemicals that are not available to the general public to control dyes or to remove spe-

Fig. 2. This Nilfisk vacuum cleaner has been fitted with a mechanism to control the strength of the vacuum suction. Small micro tools, made for cleaning computers and stereo equipment, can be attached when dealing with smaller, fragile textiles. The edges of the gray screening shown here are bound with cotton twill tape to prevent them from snagging on historic textiles. By vacuuming through screening, loose elements (such as embroidery threads or damaged warps and wefts in the weave structure) can be safely surface-cleaned without being sucked up into the hose. Many vacuum cleaners are now made with HEPA (High Efficiency Particulate Air) filters and are often recommended for people with allergies to household dust.

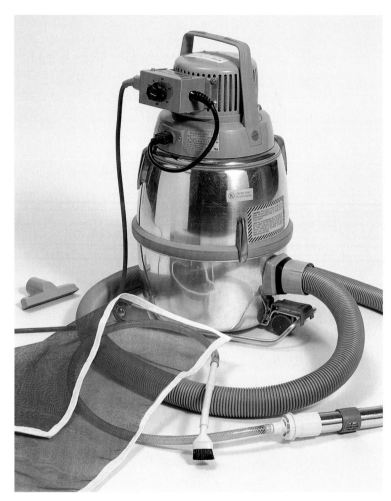

cific types of soiling. Large washing tables and adequate space for drying textiles flat allow for the cleaning of fragile textiles without folding or manipulating.

If you want to wash your historic textile yourself (knowing that it may be a risky undertaking), here are some guidelines to follow:

■   Test any colors by placing a small drop of the cleaning solution and watc-comes off, do not wash. Note that some dyes may bleed when washed even if tests indicate otherwise. You should be aware that any colored textile is at high risk.

FIG. 3. This quilt was made by Rebecca Scattergood Savery in 1827 for her daughter's wedding. A stunning example of a sunburst pattern, it is made of 6,708 pieces of printed cotton. The quilt is in excellent condition. It was likely kept in storage as the wedding never took place. The original glaze on the fabric survives because the quilt has never been washed. It is particularly important to prevent this quilt from getting dirty. Cleaning it would diminish both its historical and monetary value.

- Use distilled water, if not for the whole process then at least for the rinsing stages.

- Wash all historic textiles by hand in a large basin or bathtub; never use a washing machine.

- Lift the textile in and out of the bath on a clean piece of screening or netting.

- Use a cleaning agent obtained from one of the companies on the List of Suppliers rather than a commercial laundry detergent.

- Dry flat textiles face down on a smooth surface and cover with clean cotton sheeting.

- Stuff three-dimensional pieces to shape with lots of soft netting to avoid the need to iron (the heat and pressure of an iron can cause significant damage).

- Be very careful. When in doubt, get professional advice.

◌ *Mounting for Display*

Mounting techniques can be as variable as textiles themselves. People often ask how to properly and safely mount and frame embroideries and hang quilts for display. Many frame shops now use acid-free materials for their framing. But textiles need to be mounted carefully to prepare them for framing. The best method is to use acid-free mount board or acid-free corrugated card and Coroplast (see List of Suppliers). The board is padded with needle-punched polyester felt, although heavy flannel can also be used. The padded board is next covered with fabric, usually cotton, that is sympathetic in appearance to the textile being mounted. These display fabrics should be washed and dried before use. The textile is then carefully stitched to the padded, covered board *(fig. 4)*.

In the past, conservators recommended that needlework be removed from original mounts (usually wooden strainers or shingles) that cause deterioration. More recently, collectors and curators have begun to recognize both the historical and monetary advantage to pieces that are still in their original mounts. Conservators are therefore experimenting with new methods to protect such items. If you have

FIG. 4. Museums mount their small textiles using an acid-free board (in this case a corrugated conservation board) covered with needle-punched polyester felt (the white underlayer) and finally a fabric chosen to be aesthetically pleasing under the historic textile to be mounted. The outer fabric should be prewashed to remove excess dye and unsuitable finishes. The historic textile is hand-stitched in place on this mount, which can then be framed in the normal way, using acid-free materials.

what is thought to be an original mount and frame, you should consult a professional conservator *(fig. 5)*.

Two methods for hanging quilts are often recommended: (1) putting a rod through a cloth sleeve stitched to the back of the quilt; or (2) using a hook-and-loop fastener such as Velcro *(fig. 6)*. The second method allows the quilt to be adjusted to hang as straight as possible, and it provides the best support across the top. For a hook-and-loop fastener, the soft side is stitched to twill tape by machine. The tape is then hand-stitched to the top of the quilt as shown in figure 6. The hook side can be attached to a piece of wood or directly to the wall.

Opposite page, above:

Fig. 5. This needlework picture was designed by Samuel Folwell and embroidered by Catherine Skinner Ward of Philadelphia in 1816. It is mounted on its original strainer. Fragments of a contemporary newspaper are adhered to the back. The original frame and reverse-painted glass also survive. Although the acid from wooden mounts causes damage to textiles, most of the potential damage has already occurred. It is very important that samplers and needlework not be removed from original mounts, which add to both the historic and monetary value of the object.

Opposite page, below:

Fig. 6. Most museums use a hook-and-loop fastener (the most common is called Velcro for hanging quilts and other large textiles. Cotton twill tape is machine-stitched to each edge of the soft side of the Velcro. Then the tape is hand-stitched to the historic textile, as shown. The hook side of the fastener is attached to a piece of wood (with staples), which can be attached to a wall. The use of a hook-and-loop fastener allows the quilt or textile to be adjusted. Old textiles are never straight or square and rarely hang straight.

Storage

Providing good storage is the best thing that anyone can do to preserve their collection. An understanding of the essential principles involved can help collectors arrive at common-sense solutions for their individual situations. The issues concern both the materials used to store textiles and the physical format in which the textiles are stored.

Wooden drawers and shelves can cause yellowing and embrittlement. Textiles should never be stored in direct contact with wood. Line drawers and shelves with acid-free materials, such as archival-quality boards, and change the materials when they begin to discolor. Care must be taken, however, as wool and silk can be embrittled by alkaline conditions, and buffered papers can also cause the off-setting of dyes. In these situations, clean white cotton or linen sheets can be used instead of acid-free tissue for lining drawers and shelves.

Ideally, chemically inert, acid-free materials should be used to store textiles. For smaller collections this usually means archival-quality boxes or rolls, which are available through a number of suppliers *(fig. 7)*. Textiles should be padded and/or interleaved with neutral, acid-free tissue that is really acid free and not buffered to an alkaline pH.

FIG. 7. This elaborate storage box was made specially for the early nineteenth-century doll shown. Each piece of clothing was padded to prevent sharp folds and creases; shaped enclosures were created to hold each piece in place. The safe storage of historic textiles need not be quite so elaborate; however, the principles of padding folds to prevent sharp creases and storing in acid-free materials are important.

Textiles should never be stored with sharp folds and creases. As fibers age, they become brittle and will eventually break where folded. Small textiles should be stored flat. If it is impossible to avoid folds, these items should be padded with acid-free tissue to prevent creases. Textiles should generally not be stored on top of one another. However, if space is a problem, stacked textiles should be well padded and interleaved with acid-free tissue. Store heavy textiles beneath lighter, more fragile pieces. Larger textiles can also be rolled around acid-free tubes. If acidic cardboard tubes are used, they should be covered with either Mylar or aluminum foil to prevent the migration of acids into the textile. The Mylar or foil should be covered with plenty of acid-free tissue, sheeting, or washed muslin before rolling the historic textile onto the tube. It is usually recommended that textiles be rolled with the right side outermost. As it is rolled, the object should be interleaved with acid-free tissue; more tissue and/or muslin or sheeting should be rolled around the outside. Tie it with a fairly wide twill tape.

ๆ

Textiles are extremely vulnerable to cumulative damage over time. Slow fading from light exposure, sharp creases that eventually cause splits along fold lines, and discoloration from poor storage materials are all common problems. As with all object care, preventing damage from occurring is the key.

CHAPTER 7

Photographs

DEBRA HESS NORRIS

$\mathcal{P}$hotographs document our world and the lives and times of our ancestors. Formed by the action of light upon a sensitized surface, these images can be very fragile, as many of the materials used to create photographs deteriorate over time, fading and yellowing. Because photographs generally are irreplaceable, it is important that we care for them properly.

Throughout the history of photography, a wide range of processes have been used, resulting in as many photographic end products: daguerreotypes, tintypes, albumen prints, and silver gelatin (black-and-white) and color photographic materials (prints and color transparencies). Metallic silver, platinum metal, pigments, and, most recently, organic dyes are some of the materials that have been used to absorb and scatter light, thereby creating the images that we see. These final image materials are typically suspended and protected in a transparent binder layer. Commonly used binder materials include albumen (the white of hens' eggs), collodion (a form of cellulose nitrate), and gelatin (a highly purified protein commercially manufactured from animal hides and bones). These binders are important in determining properties such as surface character, gloss, density, and color as well as the overall image stability. Nineteenth- and twentieth-century photographs may be printed on paper, glass, metal, cellulose nitrate, cellulose acetate, or polyester film. These primary support materials provide structural support for the binder layer.

♀ *Photographic Processes*

Caretakers of photographic collections should try to identify the various photographic processes represented within their collections. Identification may be informed by knowledge of the time period during which these processes were most commonly used, methods of manufacture, and primary deterioration characteristics.

The daguerreotype, the earliest photographic medium to become popular in America, was prevalent from 1840 to 1860 *(fig. 1)*. The daguerreotype is a mirror-like image. In this process, a light-sensitive silver-plated sheet of copper is exposed to light and developed over mercury vapor. The result is an image in which the whites, or highlights, are a silver-mercury-gold amalgam, and the dark image areas are pure silver metal. The daguerreotype plate is susceptible to degradation, resulting in the formation of corrosion films at the outer edges. To keep dust and fingerprints from damaging these fragile surfaces, daguerreotypes were usually sealed to a decorative brass mat and cover glass. These protective packages were then fitted into miniature cases covered with embossed leather or paper.

The albumen print, first introduced in 1850, dominated the photographic market from 1855 to 1890 *(fig. 2)*. To make an albumen print, thin, high-quality rag papers were floated on a solution of egg white that contained a small amount of sodium chloride. The albumenized paper was then made light sensitive by placing it in a silver nitrate solution. The paper was then placed in direct contact with a glass-plate negative and exposed to daylight until the image became visible. Following exposure, the image was toned with gold chloride and fixed with sodium hyposulfite to remove remaining light-reactive salts. Commercial albumen prints were typically adhered to decorative cardboard mounts that varied in size, such as the carte-de-visite (2 1/2 by 4 inches) and the cabinet card (4 1/4 by 6 1/2 inches). Albumen prints in excellent condition often appear deep purplish-brown in color. Unfortunately, the vast majority of these images have faded and yellowed due to the oxidation of their photolytic silver image and degradation of the egg-white protein. Albumen prints may be identified by this characteristic deterioration as well as their surface, which may appear somewhat cracked and crazed.

In the tintype process, which was patented in 1856 and in popular use in America throughout the rest of the nineteenth century, collodion was poured onto a sheet of black-lacquered (japanned) iron *(fig. 3)*. These tintype images lack contrast, most often appearing gray, with creamy white highlights. High relative humidity and moisture may result in severe rusting of the tintype's iron support. This is most visible at the plate's unvarnished edges or anywhere the protective, japanned surface has been damaged. Tintypes were often placed into decorative paper cards. They may be found loose or housed in Victorian photographic albums.

In 1880 the silver-gelatin photographic process was introduced. It remained popular through the 1960s *(fig. 4)*. In the early process, silver-gelatin prints were made by placing light-sensitive paper in contact with a negative and exposing it to sunlight. Like the albumen print, these images are typically warm brown in tone. Developing-out silver-gelatin papers (in common use after 1905) were exposed directly to light in an enlarger. After exposure, these photographic images were chemically developed, fixed, and washed. In good condition, these prints appear black and white in color. Their surfaces may be matte, glossy, or canvas-textured. The print may have borders and be mounted or loose in stacks. Aged silver-gelatin prints are often faded and discolored. Some deterioration and discoloration may be attributed to improper fixing and washing during processing, but considerable damage is typically caused by exposure to a poor environment and airborne pollutants. Upon exposure to these conditions, the dark areas of silver-gelatin prints maybecome highly reflective and iridescent. This is referred to as "silver mirroring."

Color photographic materials—the types of photographs that we are most familiar with today—were introduced to the commercial market in 1945. They are made of organic dyes. These images rapidly discolor and fade, creating a shift in image color to cyan (blue) or magenta (red). The decolorization of organic dyestuffs in color photographs is due to irreversible changes in their chemical structures. Upon exposure to light, high humidity, or high temperature conditions, organic dyes are irreversibly converted to colorless dye fragments. The permanence of these dyes varies with the process and is also related to conditions of storage and use.

✲ *What You Can Do*

All photographic materials are vulnerable to severe deterioration when exposed to damaging display procedures, improper storage enclosures, careless handling prac-

Above:

FIG. 1. A mirrorlike daguerreotype image of a seated woman is visible on the right side of this opened leather case. Note the highly reflective silver-plated surface and the dark silver corrosion at the outer edges of the image. The portrait on the left is an ambrotype. Similar to the tintype process and introduced in the early 1850s in America, this type of photograph is on a clear glass support and is not as reflective as the daguerreotype. The ambrotype image is deteriorated at its outer edges and has missing areas in the black lacquer layer (appearing as areas of clear glass) along the bottom edge.

Opposite page, above:

FIG. 2. Cartes-de-visite (or visiting cards) were collected and treasured during the Victorian era. "Cartomania" (1860–70) revolutionized the profession and business of photography. The cartes-de-visite pictured here are albumen prints in various states of preservation. The albumen print at the far left is in generally good condition with minimal fading and discoloration. In comparison, the baby's portrait at the far right is severely faded and yellowed. This deterioration is characteristic of the albumen process.

Opposite page, below:

FIG. 3. The tintype was in popular use in America throughout the second half of the nineteenth century. Tintypes were pasted into paper cards, housed in decorative miniature cases, or left loose for placement in albums. The tintype's support is black-lacquered iron. When exposed to high relative humidity conditions, these images will rust. Rust staining is visible on the white paper mount of the tintype in the upper far right of this illustration.

FIG. 4. These twentieth-century black-and-white, or silver gelatin, photographs are characteristically faded and yellowed. Some of this deterioration may be attributed to improper processing during their manufacture, but considerable damage has been caused by exposure to high temperature and relative humidity levels and airborne pollutants. These print materials require individual enclosures to protect them from further degradation.

tices, or inadequate environmental conditions. High temperatures and relative humidity levels combined with dirt, dust, pollutants, and pests will rapidly accelerate deterioration. A basic understanding of these factors is absolutely critical to the long-term preservation of irreplaceable photographs.

Adverse environmental conditions, such as storing collections of photographs in a basement or attic, are the primary cause of deterioration. When exposed to relative humidity levels above 60 percent, photographic images will irreversibly fade and yellow. In addition, binder layers will soften and mildew, and poor-quality mounts will deteriorate. Low relative humidity levels will cause binder layers to crack or peel. Fluctuations in temperature and humidity will cause photographs to curl and distort, and their layered structure will separate.

Most photographic collections should be housed in room-temperature conditions with a constant relative humidity of 30 to 50 percent. Avoid humidity fluctuations of more than 5 percent. An interior closet or an air-conditioned room can be an excellent storage location. Dehumidifiers and fans may be used to locally control the environment. Cold storage (temperatures of 40°F or lower) is the only way to preserve color photographs in their original form for long periods of time. Low-temperature storage may be impractical, but collections may be packaged in polyethylene bags and vapor-proof containers for storage in frost-free refrigerators or chest freezers. Consult a photographic conservator for specific details.

Exposure to visible light is damaging to photographic materials. Following light exposure, paper supports may become brittle, and binder layers, especially albumen, will yellow and stain. The hand-colored surfaces of daguerreotypes and tintypes (where red pigment is often added to a sitter's cheeks to make them appear "lifelike") and the dyed fabric interiors of miniature cases are susceptible to severe fading. Extended display, especially under bright ultraviolet-rich sunlight, will destroy color prints.

Framed photographs should not be hung on exterior walls or in direct sunlight. When possible, incandescent light (for example, spot tungsten lights) should be used. For additional protection, windows should be covered with shades, blinds, or drapes. Ultraviolet-filtering Plexiglas will provide some protection from light and will not shatter if a picture falls. Likewise, photographs should not be framed directly against glass or Plexiglas. Prints must be properly matted with acid-free materials. Depending on the type, condition, and format of the print, paper photo corners or lightweight paper hinges may be used to secure the photograph into the window mat. This should be done by an experienced framer or under the direction of a conservation professional.

Permanent exhibition is not recommended. The effects of light are cumulative. If you wish to display a photograph for an extended period of time, consider having a duplicate or copy made. The original may then be stored properly and preserved.

Protective high-quality paper or plastic enclosures will ensure that photographs are not damaged by dirt, dust, and pollutants that can abrade images, deposit contaminants, and accelerate image fading and deterioration *(fig. 5)*. Such enclosures not only will provide additional physical support but also may serve as an effective and inexpensive buffer between the photograph and severe environmental fluctuations.

The best enclosure materials are constructed from chemically stable plastic or paper without sulfur, acids, and peroxides. Acidic paper envelopes, polyvinyl chloride (PVC) plastic (often identified by its strong odor), rubber bands, metal clips, and poor-quality adhesives, such as rubber cement and pressure-sensitive tapes, must be avoided. Acid-free paper storage enclosures are available in many forms and standard sizes (see List of Suppliers). Select paper enclosures that have passed the American National Standards Institute Photographic Activity Test (PAT). The PAT determines whether there will be harmful chemical or physical interactions between a photograph and its enclosure over its storage lifetime. This information should be provided by the manufacturer.

Both buffered and unbuffered stock may be used safely. However, buffered storage enclosures are not recommended for the long-term protection of cyanotypes or contemporary color prints because their image materials may be adversely affected. Paper enclosures are opaque, easy to label (use pencil and avoid ink), and affordable.

Plastic enclosure materials that are suitable include uncoated polyester film, polyethylene, and polypropylene. These plastics are recommended because of their exceptional long-term stability. The use of plastic enclosures may greatly minimize direct handling, as images can be viewed easily.

Airborne pollutants will cause photographic images to fade and discolor. Gaseous by-products given off by fresh oil-based paint fumes, plywood, deteriorated cardboard, and many cleaning solutions may accelerate image degradation.

FIG. 5. Photographic prints should be housed in protective enclosures and boxed to protect them from dirt, dust, pollutants, and handling-related damage. These photographic prints have been placed in inert polyester film sleeves that allow the images to be viewed easily.

Storage in acid-free enclosures and containers will help protect images from the damaging effects of these airborne pollutants.

Matted and sleeved photographs should be housed in acid-free boxes, such as those sold by most conservation supply companies (see List of Suppliers). Paper and board stock used to construct these storage boxes may be buffered. Be sure that all folders and enclosures fit the inner dimensions of the storage box so that they will stack neatly and not shift dangerously. If they are generally in good condition, photographs measuring 10 by 12 inches or smaller can be housed upright in boxes or in acid-free hanging file folders. Boxes and cabinets must not be overcrowded but also must not be so loosely filled that all support is lost. Equip vertical file drawers with upright supports of acid-free board every 6 inches.

Place early miniature-cased photographs, including daguerreotypes and tintypes, into small protective boxes or acid-free paper envelopes and house flat. Keep loose tintypes in polyester sleeves or, if flaking is present, in paper enclosures *(fig. 6)*.

Albums may be used to store and organize photographic collections. Many commercially available albums are made from good-quality materials and can be purchased from conservation supply companies. At all times, avoid the use of albums constructed of highly colored pages. Never use commercially available magnetic or "no-stick" albums for the storage of treasured photographs. These materials will deteriorate quickly over time; adhesives will yellow and fail or become completely intractable.

Photographs should be handled with care. Carelessness may result in permanent tears, cracks, losses, abrasions, fingerprints, and stains. Resist the common temptation to sort through piles of photographs, and do not touch their surfaces directly if they are unprotected. The salts in human perspiration can quickly damage and etch the delicate surfaces of photographs and cause image materials to fade. Wear white cotton gloves when working with collections that are not protected by enclosures and when handling photographs that require temporary removal from paper or plastic sleeves. Damaged and deteriorated photographs, mounted on potentially acidic and brittle mounts, must be carefully supported during handling to avoid breakage.

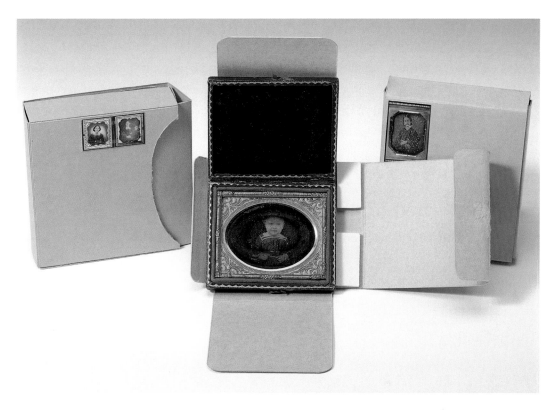

FIG. 6. Early miniature-cased photographs (such as the daguerreotype pictured here) should be housed in acid-free protective boxes and stored flat. Black-and-white contact prints showing the contents of each box will minimize handling. Display of these materials should be kept to a minimum, as the textile and leather components and image handcoloring (if present) may fade irreversibly upon exposure to light.

When to Call a Professional

Conservation treatment may be necessary for some deteriorated photographic materials. To develop a suitable preservation plan, a photograph conservator must take into consideration the chemical composition and physical condition of the deteriorated photograph as well as the immediate and long-term risks and merits of a particular treatment procedure. Further considerations are the purpose (exhibition versus storage) and scope (single item versus large group) of these interventions. Practical, reversible, and predictable conservation treatment procedures for deteriorated photographic print materials are continually being developed and refined.

Photographs that may require treatment most urgently include those that exhibit active mold growth, flaking binder layers, degraded pressure-sensitive and rubber cement adhesives, and severely embrittled primary and secondary supports. Methods for the chemical restoration of faded photographs are currently unreliable and undergoing further research. In some cases, severely faded and discolored images can be photographically or digitally copied for enhanced image resolution. Under no circumstances should attempts be made to remove disfiguring corrosion from a daguerreotype's surface, as some cleaning procedures will permanently alter its chemical and physical properties. These treatments, like those for photographic prints, must be undertaken by a trained photograph conservator.

৯১

A general understanding of the nature of photographic materials—their final image materials, binders, and primary supports—will provide a solid basis for developing a practical collection preservation strategy. Many factors, including environmental conditions, storage and exhibition procedures, and handling practices, will directly influence the permanence of these materials. These factors must be regularly monitored, evaluated, and controlled if we are to preserve these irreplaceable images for the enrichment, education, and enjoyment of future generations.

CHAPTER 8

Metals

MARGARET A. LITTLE

Since ancient times, metal has been used to fabricate objects for everyday use, implements of war, tokens to mark occasions of personal or social importance, and items with no other purpose than to delight the owner. The physical properties of metal, its malleability and ductility in particular, allow it to be worked in a wide variety of ways. This adaptability and the overall strength of metal once it has been formed into an object may account for its long history of use.

ꙮ *Nature of the Materials*

Except for gold, which can be found in a pure state in nature, the metal used to fabricate both utilitarian and decorative arts objects is mined as an ore. The ore must then be refined to extract the metal. Once refined, the metal is typically mixed with one or more other metals to form an alloy that has the desirable characteristics of its constituent parts. For example, gold can be mixed with silver or copper to create an alloy that has the color of gold but is harder and more durable than unalloyed gold. Some of the more common alloys and their major constituents are sterling silver (a combination of 92.5 percent silver and 7.5 percent copper); brass (copper and zinc); bronze (copper and tin); iron/steel (iron and carbon); nickel silver or German silver (copper, nickel, and zinc); pewter (tin and lead); and Britannia (tin, copper, and antimony). Other metals may also be present in these alloys in small amounts.

♀ *Fabrication*

The methods used to make metal objects fall into two main categories: hand fabrication and casting. Within these two categories there are a wide range of techniques; sometimes more than one technique will be used to create an object *(fig. 1)*. Included in the category of hand-fabrication techniques are sinking or raising a three-dimensional shape from a flat sheet of metal using hammers; building a three-dimensional shape by assembling flat pieces of metal; bending sheets of metal; forging metal rods; and twisting or weaving wire. These basic methods are also used in industry, but the process is expedited with machinery. If an object is cast, a mold made of sand, plaster, metal, or silicone rubber is created from a model. Molten metal is then poured into the mold. When the metal has hardened, the mold is removed.

As there are many methods of fabricating metal objects, so there are various ways to decorate their surfaces *(fig. 2)*. Perhaps the simplest technique involves polishing the surface to a bright, mirrorlike finish. A surface can also be engraved, etched, or stamped with a design. Three-dimensional designs can be created by hammering recesses and high points into the metal—called *chasing* and *repoussé*.

The surface of metal can be changed in a number of ways to create decorative finishes. Paint or colored lacquers can be applied in simple or elaborate patterns. The natural colors of metal can also be changed through the application of a variety of chemicals, in a technique called *patination*. For example, the natural orange/red color of copper can be turned black, gray, red, blue, or green depending on the chemical it is exposed to. Such color exists as a thin film on the surface of the object and can be quite delicate and prone to abrasion and loss.

Another way to change the surface characteristics of a metal object is through *plating*. Using this technique, a thin layer of one metal is applied to another. Usually, a more precious metal (gold or silver) is applied over silver, copper, iron, or pewter. As with patinated decoration, plating can be easily worn or abraded.

The last category of decoration found on metal objects involves the addition of elements: these can be metallic, such as the cast decorative elements found on the

FIG. 1. Often, a number of manufacturing techniques are used to fabricate a single metal object. The body of this tureen, cover, and stand were shaped and decorated by hammering flat sheets of silver to the desired shape. The handles, finial, and dolphin figures were cast from molten metal. The handles were then soldered to the tureen, while the finial and dolphin figures had screws soldered to them so that they could be bolted to the object.

tureen in figure 1, or nonmetallic, such as precious, semiprecious, or nonprecious stones and enameled decoration.

Deterioration

In discussing the deterioration of metal objects, two types are normally cited: physical and chemical. Physical deterioration includes such damage as dents, tears, complete or partial detachment of attached elements, loss of attached elements, scratches

Fɪɢ. 2. An enormous variety of materials and techniques have been used to decorate the surfaces of metal objects. For example, some of the copper alloy surfaces of the opium lamp *(bottom left)* were decorated with enamel (a colored glass), which was fired on the surface. The goldlike surfaces of the Argand lamp *(center)* were created by applying a tinted lacquer to the surface; the dark areas are a copper alloy treated with a chemical to create a patinated surface. Both the lacquer and patina exist as thin layers on the surface of the metal; they are fragile and vulnerable to abrasion. The iron box *(bottom right)* has a wash of tin on the surface, which has been painted. The tin is visible in areas where the paint is missing; it resembles silver.

or abrasion, or loss of plating. Physical damage usually occurs because of use, poor handling, improper storage, or the use of aggressive cleaning materials or techniques. Because metal objects appear to be so strong and durable, it is sometimes easy to forget that they can be damaged by poor handling or cleaning, the primary agents of physical deterioration *(fig. 3)*.

Chemical deterioration is also called corrosion. Everyone is familiar with the green corrosion found on the surfaces of copper and copper alloy objects, the black tarnish on silver or silver-plate objects, or the red/orange rust found on the surfaces of iron objects. Such corrosion is the visual evidence of the chemical deterioration of the metal. Corrosion is a complex process that can be caused by a variety of factors. However, it is important to understand that corrosion of metals is a natural process that begins at the moment the metal is extracted from ore. Ore is the most stable form for the material, and, by corroding, a metal is returning to this stable state. Corrosion can also be accelerated by environmental factors such as acids or other chemical pollutants in the atmosphere, materials used to store or display metal objects *(fig. 4)*, oils deposited on metal surfaces from handling, or high relative humidity levels. Conservators normally classify corrosion as being

FIG. 3. Although it appears to be a hearty material, metal is prone to physical damage, as illustrated here. The broken handle of the spoon was possibly caused by stress. The bell has been dented, possibly from being struck by another object.

active (the corrosion process is causing continuing loss of material) or inactive (a stable oxide layer forms on the surface that sometimes acts as a protective patina).

℘ What You Can Do

For the collector of metal objects, the most important step in preservation is preventing deterioration before it happens. Physical deterioration can be averted or at least minimized by establishing proper handling procedures and selecting appropriate storage methods. For example, metal objects with handles, such as teapots or coffeepots, should never be picked up by their handles alone, since these are generally areas that have been stressed over the years and have become weak. The handle may give way, and the body of the piece may fall, creating dents. Instead, hold or carry an object with two hands; if the handle must be used, be sure to support the object with the other hand as a precaution. Another preventive measure is to place a cushioning material between metal objects when they are stacked and under them when they are placed on a shelf. This will prevent abrasion that might occur if the surface were to rub against another metal object or against the hard surface of the shelf. A delicate touch should be used when cleaning metal objects to pre-

Fɪɢ. 4. Exposure to an acidic material caused the patterned corrosion seen on the surface of this cup. The striped pattern suggests that the cup came into contact with a fabric of some kind. If this type of corrosion is left untreated, it causes a loss of metal; the pattern would become permanently etched into the surface of the metal. For this reason, it is important to prevent metal from corroding.

vent scratching. Even the softest cloth can cause permanent abrasion if used too aggressively. Dust should be removed by gently moving a brush or soft cloth over the surface.

Chemical deterioration is more difficult to prevent, but measures can be taken to slow its progress. First, it is recommended that metal objects be handled with gloves (cotton or latex gloves are best) to prevent corrosion caused by the deposit of hand oils on the metal surface. If these areas are not cleaned, the metal can become permanently etched. Second, care should be used in choosing the materials that come into contact or close proximity with the metal object. Materials such as plastics, paints, and fabrics contain elements that can give off harmful vapors as they age, creating a corrosive environment for the metal object. For example, the wool sometimes found in the felt that lines silverware drawers contains sulfur, which will tarnish silver and silver-plate objects. Plastics made with polyvinyl chloride (PVC) tend to give off chloride vapors as they age, which combine with atmospheric water to form hydrochloric acid, a very corrosive chemical for all metals. In general, it is best to use storage materials purchased from specialized suppliers or materials that are labeled "acid free" or "archival" (see List of Suppliers).

Last, it is important that metal objects be kept in a stable environment—one that is free from atmospheric pollutants and where the temperature and relative humidity are kept within a certain range. For general collections, a range of 40 percent (plus or minus 5 percent) relative humidity and 68°F (plus or minus two degrees) is recommended. Specialized collections, such as archaeological bronzes, may require a much lower relative humidity environment. As noted previously, atmospheric pollutants can cause corrosion of metal objects. Temperature and relative humidity also play a key role. Elevated relative humidity can initiate some corrosion processes, and elevated temperature can cause corrosive reactions to accelerate. The following sections outline actions an individual collector can take to help preserve objects made of a specific metal or alloy.

Gold

Gold itself is one of the most stable metals. However, the metals that are alloyed with gold may corrode, depositing corrosion products on the surface of the gold object. In such a situation, it is tempting to remove the offending corrosion to reveal the gold. However, it would be advisable to consult with a conservator first, as the gold may be scratched in the process of removing corrosion. If the surface of a gold object is obscured only with dirt and grime, it is possible to clean it with a soft brush or a small amount of ethyl alcohol on a cotton swab. Because gold is so soft, a gold object is much more likely to suffer physical damage, such as abrasion or denting. To prevent physical damage, careful handling procedures must be followed.

℘   *Silver and Silver-Plate Objects*

Silver, like gold, is a soft metal and is prone to abrasion and denting if not handled carefully. This is true even when the silver is alloyed with another metal. The silver plating on objects can be even more prone to abrasion since it exists as a thin layer on the surface of the metal. Therefore, care should be taken in the handling and storage of these objects. In cleaning, only the gentlest techniques and materials should be used. Simple dust, dirt, and grease can be removed with a soft brush or ethyl alcohol on a cotton swab.

The most common problem found with silver or silver-plate objects is tarnish—the black film that forms over the silver. In most cases, tarnish can be removed using a mild abrasive (see sidebar on tarnish removal, p. 100). When this mixture is gently rubbed over the surface of tarnished silver, the tarnish is removed. Commercial silver polishes are not recommended since they can contain harsh chemicals that, if not completely removed, can cause further corrosion.

Before embarking on any cleaning regimen, it is important to understand how the metal object—be it silver, gold, copper alloy, or iron—was fabricated and decorated, since any action taken to clean the object can cause irreversible damage. The black surface on a silver object might be an intentionally applied patina, not tarnish, and if it is carelessly removed in cleaning, the intrinsic nature of the object will be altered and its monetary value can be affected.

℘   *Copper and Copper Alloys*

In its pure state, copper is a soft metal that can be easily deformed or abraded. Depending on the metal added to copper, its alloys have a range of hardness and color. However, no matter the composition, a copper alloy can still be abraded.

Copper and copper alloy metals are also prone to corrosion, caused by the presence of ammonia, acids, alkalis, chlorides, and sulfide gasses. The same prohibitions discussed for the cleaning of silver and silver-plate objects exist for copper and copper alloy objects. The removal of simple dirt, dust, and grime can be accomplished with a soft brush or with ethyl alcohol on a cotton swab.

There are times when it is inappropriate to remove dirt, grime, or even corrosion. On some archaeological copper alloy objects, for example, corrosion that is not actively causing deterioration of the object is thought to be desirable and is often not removed.

≈ Pewter

Pewter is a soft metal alloy that can easily be dented, deformed, and abraded. Lead, one of the metals in the pewter alloy, is very reactive and prone to corrosion. Normally an oxide film forms on the surface of pewter, which causes it to become dull. In this case, the oxide film is thought to act as a protective layer, preventing further corrosion of the metal; it is generally not removed. Lead is easily corroded by organic acids, which can be found in such materials as wood, paints, and varnishes—materials that are frequently found in storage and display cabinets. In the presence of organic acids, a white corrosion will form on pewter. Dirt, dust, and grime can be removed with a soft brush or with ethyl alcohol on a cotton swab. Because pewter is so soft, only gentle pressure should be used when cleaning.

≈ Iron

Iron is perhaps the most ubiquitous metal in collections; it is also the most problematic in terms of care. Iron is sensitive to elevated relative humidity and acidic environments and can very quickly begin to corrode. Maintaining a low relative humidity and a nonacidic environment is perhaps the most critical step for the preservation of iron objects.

Beyond simple dusting to remove dirt and grime, the collector should exercise great caution before attempting to clean iron objects. Iron objects can be plated (tin is a commonly found plating metal) or painted. It would be easy to unintentionally remove the plating or paint with a cleaning solution, even one as mild as ethyl alcohol.

ِ٭   *When to Call a Professional*

If a metal object requires more than simple cleaning—that is, the removal of dirt, dust, and grime from the surface or tarnish removal from silver or silver-plate surfaces—a conservator should be contacted. Metal is a complicated material, and the preservation issues for metal objects are equally complicated. For example, it is possible that a painted or gilded surface exists under the dirt and corrosion seen on the object in figure 5. If the object were not carefully examined prior to cleaning, the underlying surface could be damaged or lost. Often, the monetary and historic significance of an object is diminished if these kinds of surface details are removed.

Objects conservators work with all types of three-dimensional objects and normally work with metal objects. Metal objects can fit into a number of different categories (decorative arts, archaeological, or historic objects), and objects conservators sometimes choose to specialize in one particular category. After making initial contact, establish a dialogue with the conservator. Ask about their experience and area of specialization; voice your expectations for the treatment; let them know if you need help with issues relating to the storage and display

TARNISH REMOVAL FROM SILVER OR SILVER-PLATE OBJECTS

1. Clean the surface of the object in water containing a few drops of a mild dishwashing detergent. Use a soft cotton flannel cloth to gently clean the surface of the object.

2. Make a slurry of precipitated calcium carbonate and ethyl alcohol or water; the mix should have a creamy consistency. Calcium carbonate should be purchased at a chemical supply firm to ensure that it is finely ground; large grains or contaminants in the calcium carbonate could scratch the metal surface. Using a cotton flannel cloth, gently rub the mixture over the metal surface. Only the gentlest pressure should be used, as it is possible to scratch the metal surface or remove plating from the object if cleaning is too vigorous. As the cotton flannel becomes dirty, change to another part of the cloth or use a fresh one.

3. Allow the mixture to dry on the object. Remove the powder residue with a clean cotton flannel cloth and soft brush.

of the object; and be sure you understand the steps in the treatment they are recommending. Also let the conservator know if the object is a functional one (such as a teapot that is still used) or decorative. Such a determination may affect the type of treatment that a conservator recommends.

A conservator will prepare a report on the examination of the object as well as a proposal for treatment, outlining the work to be done. If you agree to the treatment, you should also receive a report documenting the work, accompanied by photographs that illustrate the condition of the object before, during, and after treatment.

FIG. 5. This oil lamp from Nepal dates from the sixteenth to seventeenth centuries. The dirt and corrosion on the surface might be considered an important interpretative feature of the object or an element that enhances its value. Removing the dirt and corrosion could devalue the object aesthetically and monetarily.

In the treatment of metal objects, conservators strive to use materials that have good aging properties (that is, they have good longevity and will not harm the object as they age) and are reversible. Such procedures ensure that treatments do no additional damage to the object and, if necessary, can be undone in the future.

One treatment an objects conservator may suggest to prevent chemical deterioration of a metal objects is the application of a protective coating to the surface. The materials used for coating metals generally are microcrystalline wax, acrylic resins, or nitrocellulose lacquer. Figure 6 illustrates how effective a coating can be in preventing tarnish on a silver object. However, some collectors do not like the aesthetic appearance of an object with a coating. They feel it compromises the metallic luster of the object and so choose not to pursue this option.

ה

The most important step you can take to ensure the preservation of any collection is to create a safe display and storage environment—one that will not cause further deterioration of the objects. Second, appropriate handling procedures must be followed. And finally, learn what preservation steps you can carry out yourself and when it is best to contact a professional. Diligence and care will result in the long-term preservation of any object or collection.

Fig. 6. The corrosion of metal can be caused by many things—atmospheric pollutants, exposure to acidic storage materials, and contact with acidic oils from skin. For this reason, many museums and collectors choose to apply a lacquer coating to metal surfaces. This silver pendant has been stored in a jeweler's box. Half of the pendant was coated with a nitrocellulose lacquer to protect the metal from the harmful vapors emanating from the materials lining the box. Within two days, the uncoated surface had tarnished while the lacquered surface was unchanged.

Works of Art on Paper

JOHN KRILL AND BETTY FISKE

Original prints, posters, or drawings are generally referred to as works of art on paper. These range from watercolor and pastel images and woodblock prints to trip souvenirs and even pictures drawn by a child. Very often, we frame and display these paper objects, whether for aesthetic or sentimental reasons. Perhaps it is not surprising then that two of the biggest problems for works of art on paper are the materials that house them and the environment. Temperature, humidity, light, and adjacent materials all pose a threat to paper objects. To better understand these problems, you must first understand the nature of paper itself.

❧ Nature of the Materials

In papermaking, a fine screen is passed through a mixture of fibers in water. The water drains through the screen, leaving a felted sheet of fibers on top of the screen. Alterations to parts of the papermaking process result in papers of differing qualities and characteristics. For example, fiber selection will determine whether you get a white writing paper, a brown wrapping paper, or numerous other paper and board types. The beating procedures used on the fibers can produce papers of regular or irregular consistency. Varying the added amount of a water-resisting agent called *size* will determine whether the papers are soft and yielding (perfect for printmaking) or firm (excellent for writing). The surface of paper may range from rough and coarse to smooth as glass. Artists are sensitive to all of these properties and select specific papers to meet their needs.

Historically, Western prints have been made with oil-based ink (rather than water-based ink) on paper that contains a small amount of sizing. Such paper has little resistance to moisture and yields easily when dampened, making it excellent for printing. This property of moisture absorption may make the paper very good for the printmaker, but it can be problematic for the owner. These papers can readily absorb moisture from the air and distort, or they can even grow mold if the moisture is present for some time.

Linen fibers were the most common material for making paper in Europe and the United States until the early nineteenth century, when cotton also was used. However, linen and cotton became harder to come by as the demand for paper grew. To solve the problem, wood fibers were successfully introduced to papermaking during the mid nineteenth century to keep paper production moving and prices low. If not highly processed, however, wood fibers introduce impurities to paper—particularly lignin, a substance that is chemically unstable. Linen, cotton, and wood share an important characteristic: they all contain cellulose, the primary substance that gives paper its properties. To understand paper in its simplest form is to understand cellulose and its strong affinity for water.

Water and Relative Humidity

In caring for paper, it soon becomes apparent that water, in either the liquid or vapor state, can be problematic. Paper quickly absorbs water and can produce dark lines of discoloration or planar distortion, such as *cockling*. Paper's attraction to water is possibly more dangerous in the vapor state than in the liquid. Water vapor is less commonly seen; here lies its danger. What is not seen is often out of mind. High humidity levels cause injury to paper and may dramatically shorten its life. Humidity levels above 65 or 70 percent encourage microbiological attack. These growths include mold—which might resemble what grows on old food—and *foxing*, a term used for the irregular reddish-brown spots found on some papers *(fig. 1)*. Many insects that eat paper also thrive in higher relative humidity. Silverfish, for example, live very comfortably in moist environments in the 70°F range.

Moisture, too, can cause paper to be physically disfigured through dimensional change, since paper expands while taking in the water. If the edges of paper are held down—such as in a mat or picture frame—the central area can cockle or bow in a moist atmosphere. Conversely, paper can shrink, giving off water to a dry atmosphere. This may also lead to distortion. Paper's association with water therefore makes it a potentially mobile material. Aim for a stable relative humidity between 40 and 50 percent.

FIG. 1. This print shows some of the effects of high humidity: cockling and foxing (brown spots). The cockling occurred because the edges of the print were held down while the rest was free to expand in the humid environment. Moisture also provided a favorable ground for the microbiological attack that resulted in the foxing.

ʂ *Heat*

Some scientists consider heat to be one of paper's biggest enemies because it breaks down cellulose and accelerates chemical reactions. Paper scientists tell us that the material is so affected by heat that its chemical reaction rates double for about every 10°F rise in temperature. A "healthy" sheet of paper stored at 68°F will lose half of its strength in 490 years. The same paper stored just nine degrees higher—at 77°F—will lose half its life in 204 years. A stable temperature of 68°F to 70°F is often recommended for paper being stored where people live or work. Cooler temperatures will greatly help preserve paper.

ʂ *Acids and Light*

Two other broad categories that strongly affect the stability of paper are acids and light. Acids may occur in paper from its manufacture, such as the presence of lignin, but acids may also be present in the environment. They can come from far away—such as air pollutants—or from close at hand—such as a wooden backing support for a framed print. Yellowing, discoloration, and embrittlement are some of the outward signs of acid attack on paper, which leads to the breakdown of cellulose and in turn the shortening of the paper's length and the diminishing of its strength.

Light causes the oxidation of cellulose, which causes paper to discolor and weaken. Have you ever noticed how colored advertising images often turn blue in sunny shop windows? The power of light can fade colors as well as injure paper (*figs. 2–5*).

Opposite and following pages:

FIGS. 2–5. These four images were originally published in a book in 1820. Figures 2 and 4 are still in the book; they maintain a fresh appearance. Figures 3 and 5—removed, framed, and hung in bright light—demonstrate well the destructive power of light. Their colors have faded, and the paper has been damaged. The paper of figure 3 was bleached by the light and contrasts with the brown discoloration at the edges caused by an acidic, poor-quality window mat. Figure 5 must have been located in brighter light because the paper, once bleached, has now turned brown from deterioration. The area exposed to light almost matches the brown deterioration caused by the acidic window mat.

FIG. 2

FIG. 3

Painted by J. Shaw.   *Engraved by J. Hill.*

WASHINGTON'S SEPULCHRE MOUNT VERNON

Published by M. Carey & Son Philadelphia.

FIG. 4

Painted by J. Shaw.   Engraved by J. Hill.

WASHINGTON'S SEPULCHRE MOUNT VERNON

Published by M. Carey & Son Philadelphia.

FIG. 5

◌ *Looking for Trouble*

When looking at paper, we can generally find clues that provide insight into the nature of potential problems or damage. Discoloration and staining are two obvious harbingers of trouble. Overall yellowing or mottling may indicate undesirable environmental exposure to one or several adverse conditions, such as light, heat, humidity, and acidity. Localized discoloration may indicate the accidental introduction of moisture or liquids from leaks or spills (and possibly subsequent mold attack to the moist paper). Or it may suggest contact with a foreign substance when the paper was laid on an unclean surface. Interestingly, some of the very materials we use to house and hypothetically protect our paper objects are, in fact, the very things that damage them.

Store-bought adhesives are so troublesome that it is safe to say that nearly all are problematic to the stability of paper. Animal glue, rubber cement, and cellulose nitrate–based glues all discolor paper. The staining may often look like brushstrokes or dabbing marks. Rectangular yellow or brown marks may indicate the presence of pieces of pressure-sensitive tapes with rubber-based adhesive, such as Scotch and masking tape *(fig. 6)*. These tapes discolor and stain paper and become brittle. Gummed linen or paper tapes, often used by framers, are less offensive but may in time cause problems, such as distortion from shrinkage of the gum. Even archival, pressure-sensitive tapes labeled "acid free" can physically distort paper and can be difficult to remove over time.

Heat-activated dry-mounting tissues have varied in composition, stability, and reversibility over the past century. Further, drymounting gives an unnatural restraint to paper. Flaws in the attachment of the drymount may leave pockets of air or creases, and these unattached areas may respond to changes in humidity and create stress within the paper.

Acidic matting and framing materials are responsible for much damage. Poor quality wood-pulp mats release acids that discolor paper. One clue to their presence is a brown "mat burn" line inside the cut window edge. Brown corrugated cardboard, if made from poor-quality wood pulp, causes even, striated, brown markings where it touches the paper. Wooden backing boards are particularly aggressive in oxidizing paper and cause brown stains that conform to the wood grain and knotholes.

FIG. 6.   The brown rectangles in the upper left corner of this lithograph were caused by Scotch tape that had been applied to mend a tear. Never use any pressure-sensitive tape on artwork. It causes discoloration, chemical injury, and physical distortion.

What You Can Do

Paper has survived for centuries—some varieties, of course, better than others. We have it in our power to care for paper. We know its simple needs. The initial quality of a paper will influence dramatically how well it can survive adverse conditions.

Art on paper should be handled as little as possible. Clean hands are essential since fingerprints may deposit soil, acids, and oils that will discolor paper and leave nutrients that attract mold or insects. Whenever possible, unmatted paper should be handled on another larger piece of clean, good-quality, sturdy paper or paperboard. Move paper by lifting it; never slide one sheet across another. Mishandling can damage paper instantly. Tears are physically irreversible; it is nearly impossible to disguise such injury completely, although a conservator may be able to stabilize the damage and make it less apparent.

Works of art on paper need to be examined periodically for visible changes; the stability of the environment in which they are housed should be monitored regularly. In the average home, maintaining low lighting conditions in display locations requires careful consideration, and displays should be changed periodically. Always remember the rather horrifying fact that the deterioration caused by light will continue even after the paper has been removed from the light and stored in the dark. Works of art on paper present a real dilemma. They are part of the visual arts, yet we must treat them with great care in order to see and preserve them. Draw blinds; pull curtains; use indirect light. These are simple, commonsense steps that can help prolong the life of paper.

℘   *Matting and Framing*

Among the most valuable steps an owner can take to protect art on paper is to properly frame and store it. Once a print or drawing has been framed or placed in a storage container, it tends to remain there for years. This makes the investment in quality archival framing and storage materials critical. These readily available products have a major impact on preservation (see List of Suppliers). Paper and paperboard products are considered archival if they are acid-free and lignin-free. Many archival products are called *buffered* papers and boards because an alkaline material, such as calcium carbonate, has been added to the board to prolong its life. Although buffered materials can enhance care, alkaline materials may also affect the media. Select a framer who is aware of these materials and who uses proper museum framing and storage techniques.

A generally accepted method of matting involves the preparation of a window mat and back mat that are cut to fit the frame. The primary purpose of a window-mat is to separate the surface of the art from the glass, thus preventing it from sticking to the glass under conditions of high or prolonged humidity. A mat thickness of at least 4-ply is recommended; large or dimensional artwork may require a much deeper recess. Clearly, the proportion, color, and decorative finish of the window mat also represent an important aesthetic choice in the presentation of the artwork. A large selection of archival mat boards is available to serve these needs.

Supplies for attaching paper are available through archival supply companies (see List of Suppliers). Paper is generally attached to a mat with hinges or corners (*fig. 7*). Pure fiber Japanese tissues, which are thin but strong, are most often used for hinges. Wheat starch paste or a methylcellulose is used to attach the hinge to the artwork and to the back mat. Common commercial adhesives and pressure-sensitive tapes, such as clear gift-wrapping tape, should never be used. Securing the art to the back mat with archival paper or Mylar corners is one alternative to hinges.

With certain works of art, a window mat is not appropriate. In such cases, the object should be hinged to a back mat and framed with a spacer between the art and the glass. Spacers are useful for oversize or dimensional objects.

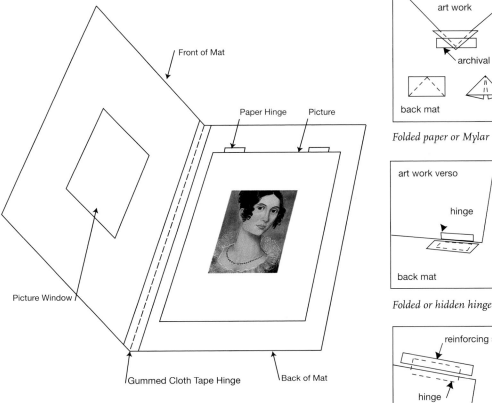

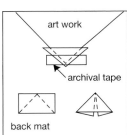

Folded paper or Mylar corner

Folded or hidden hinge

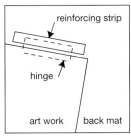

Reinforced hanging hinge

FIG. 7. To properly mat and frame a work of art on paper, use acid-free and lignin-free materials around the object. Paper can be safely attached to the mat using corners or hinges.

There are a number of choices, in addition to glass, for use in framing. Single-weight "picture" glass is the norm. Another option is acrylic sheeting, such as Plexiglas and Lucite, which is both nonbreakable and generally lighter than glass and can be advantageous when shipping artwork. Ultraviolet-filtering acrylic sheets are available and may help slow the fading of some sensitive colored media. However, do not be overconfident. All light, including the visible light we see, can injure works of art on paper.

The delicate surfaces of pastel and charcoal drawings and papers with strong, three-dimensional qualities are best protected through storage in frames. However, you may not want to mat and frame everything. Prints, watercolors, and pencil-and-ink drawings may also be stored safely in archival paper folders (see List of Suppliers). These can be laid flat in archival boxes or in metal flat files. If you place more than one artwork within a folder, separate each piece with a sheet of acid-free paper.

꩜   *When to Call a Professional*

A responsible owner resists the temptation to try complex conservation procedures. Irreparable damage can be done by attempting to conserve valuable art on paper without the necessary experience. Consult a trained professional conservator who can assess and treat your objects. Place a damaged object in an archival folder until it can be treated. Never attempt a repair using a pressure-sensitive tape.

Like people, works of art on paper like to be comfortable. For paper, the preference is to be cool rather than warm, dry rather than damp, and shaded rather than exposed to direct light. Thoughtful display and storage in archival, acid-free, and lignin-free materials are critical. Paper should be handled only one way: with care.

CHAPTER 10

Paintings

MARK F. BOCKRATH

Paintings range in intention and use from decorative and functional objects, such as firescreens, to "fine art" easel paintings; they also vary widely in their materials and construction. Painting types include fresco (on wet plaster), egg tempera on panels, and oil or acrylic emulsions on fabric. The support of a painting (such as fabric, paper, a wooden panel, or fabricated board) and the nature of the paints determine the appearance and surface character of a painting. The artist's use of these methods and materials can determine a painting's longevity *(fig. 1)*.

❧ *The Construction of Paintings*

Paintings are complex structures. Since collectors are generally concerned with easel paintings and decorative painted wooden artifacts rather than frescoes, this chapter concentrates on the structure of a typical easel painting on fabric or panel *(fig. 2)*.

The support for a typical easel painting can be a wooden or fiberboard panel or a fabric, such as linen or cotton, that is stretched on an expandable, wooden frame called a *stretcher* or on a fixed frame called a *strainer*. A stretched canvas can be expanded with a wooden key, which is hammered into the stretcher's corner joints, thereby increasing its dimensions and tightening the fabric. Tacks or staples are used to attach the fabric to the stretcher at the edges. This foundation is then coated

Fig. 1. This nineteenth-century American painting received recent conservation treatment, bringing it much closer to its original appearance.

with a thin layer of animal skin glue or acrylic emulsion. This coating, or *size*, layer makes the panel or fabric less absorbent and prepares it for the application of a priming, or ground, layer.

The ground layer for traditional panel paintings is a smooth, white gesso film consisting of multiple layers of a water-based glue and chalk mixture. The traditional ground layer for a stretched fabric consists of a drying oil and pigments that range in color from white or pale cream and gray to deep brown or red. Recently, synthetic grounds of "acrylic gesso" have been widely used. Traditional gesso is brittle and therefore was rarely used on fabric; gesso, oil, or synthetic ground layers can all be used on wooden panels.

Paint is applied to the ground layer after the artist completes an underdrawing in ink, charcoal, or pencil. The paint consists of colored pigments of mineral, organic, or synthetic origin mixed with sticky binders, such as oil, egg yolk, or synthetic emulsions. Egg tempera paintings are built up with thin, transparent washes of color or densely hatched opaque films of pigment and egg. Oil and acrylic paintings can be applied directly—in a wet-into-wet technique or interlayered with opaque colors—or indirectly—with thin, transparent glazes of medium-rich color over a dried underpainting. Some paintings combine both indirect and direct techniques or incorporate different paint media within the painting's design.

Traditional paintings usually are coated with a layer of varnish, which protects the paint surface from moisture, scratches, and grime and provides color saturation and an even gloss to the paint surface. Varnishes such as *mastic* and *damar* consist of tree resins dissolved in solvents and have served as surface coatings for centuries. More recent varnish resins are synthetic in manufacture and include acrylic and ketone resins.

Paintings and the Environment

The various components of a painting respond to the environment differently. The layers swell with a rise in relative humidity and contract at low relative humidity.

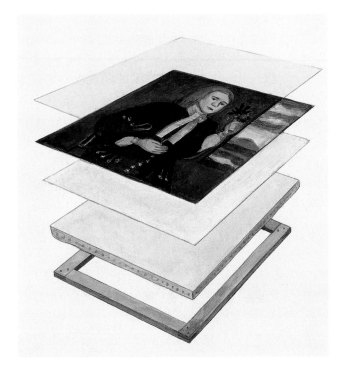

Fig. 2. This drawing illustrates the layered structure of a painting on fabric, showing *(from bottom to top)* the stretcher, support fabric, ground layer, actual painting, and varnish layer.

Because they do so at different rates and with differing changes in total volume, the result is an eventual loosening of the bond between the layers. As the materials in a painting age, they become brittle, and expansion and contraction may cause breakage in the paint and ground, splits in wood panels, and slackening and deterioration of fabric supports. The combined effect of the environment and age thus results in cracking, cupping, and flaking of the paint.

For the long-term preservation of paintings, it is easy to see, therefore, why it is so important to maintain a stable environment, avoiding large fluctuations in relative humidity and temperature within short periods of time. Paintings respond better to slow environmental changes than to fast ones. Prolonged exposure to low relative humidity can result in the tightening of support layers, thus stressing paint that is brittle and dry. Low relative humidity also causes wooden panels to warp and split. Prolonged exposure to high relative humidity can cause panels to warp as well and can make paintings on canvas sag and buckle. At relative humidity over 80 percent, the fabric support may shrink; at this point the fabric is so swollen with water that its weave structure changes and causes flaking. Further, excessive humidity encourages mold growth.

Lighting is another concern for the display of paintings. Allowing sunlight to shine directly onto paintings is never a good idea, as this can cause them to fade, heat up, and dry out. Indirect lighting is preferable. Sunlight and fluorescent light are high in ultraviolet light, which readily fades colors and degrades oils and fabrics. Incandescent light is lower in ultraviolet content but can still produce a great deal of heat—as seen by the cracked, flaking paint that appears in the upper central portions of paintings illuminated by picture lamps attached to the tops of their frames. These lamps should be avoided.

✥ What You Can Do

The first step in safeguarding your collection is to carefully examine each painting and record its condition in writing and photographs. This will enable you to monitor any changes in its condition over time, alert you to problems as they arise, and provide useful information to a conservator treating the painting. Note the location of tears or cracks in panels and the presence of grime or yellowed varnish. Distinguish between the types of cracks. Thin, mechanical cracks that extend through the paint and ground layers all the way to the support may result in flaking *(fig. 3)*. Drying, or "traction," cracks that are shallow and wide, revealing lower paint layers, may be disfiguring but are not insecure *(fig. 4)*.

Check to see if the painting is loose in its frame or if the tacking edges are split and insecure. Use a strong light to see detail, and hold the light at a tilted angle, parallel to the painting's surface, to more easily see lifted paint flakes or puckered canvas *(fig. 5)*. An ultraviolet lamp, commonly known as a "black light," can be useful in determining the presence of an aged, natural resin coating or repaint. Aged varnishes may appear hazy and greenish under ultraviolet light, and recent repaint may show up as black splotches scattered over damaged areas.

If the painting is not flaking, a soft, sable watercolor brush (not a feather duster) may be used to brush away loose dust. If there are unattached pieces of paint or frame ornamentation, save them. They can be reattached by a conservator, thereby retaining more original material and saving treatment time. Paintings that are severely flaking may be too delicate to display on a wall or store vertically. Store them flat until a conservator can be consulted. Tears in canvas should not be patched or glued. Surgical tape (which is easily removed) can be applied to the reverse of torn fabric to serve as a temporary mend and hold the tear flat, preventing it from worsening.

Covering the reverse of a painting with a backing of foamboard or acid-free cardboard screwed into the stretcher will protect it from damage. This will also prevent grime and debris from covering the back and accumulating between the bottom part of the stretcher and the canvas, where it can cause a bulge. A backing board can also lessen the effect of vibration on a painting during transit.

Proper framing techniques include the use of soft brass mending plates rather than nails to hold the painting in the frame *(fig. 6)*. The plates can be bent to conform to the stretcher and frame. Nails can split stretchers and restrict the movement of panels, thereby inducing stress. Gluing felt into the rabbet, or inner edge, of a frame provides a cushion for the edges of the painting and prevents abrasion of paint. Paintings on wooden panels should not be tightly mounted in a frame. They need room to move with fluctuations in relative humidity.

Hang your paintings away from vents, wet walls, radiators, fireplaces, or other hazardous locations. Apply spacing bumpers to the reverse of frames to allow air flow and discourage localized moisture buildup.

FIG. 3. In this detail of the painting *MARY NORMAN ROSE PRINCE*, mechanical cracking is visible in the paint and ground layers. The cracking has resulted from the expansion and contraction of the paint due to fluctuations in climate and may result in flaking paint.

FIG. 4. This detail of a nineteenth-century American landscape shows wide traction cracks that expose the dark underlayers of the painting. These cracks have resulted from tension in the paint due to differences in drying rates of the various layers. Such cracks may be disfiguring, but they will not flake off.

FIG. 5. (*above*) This photograph of figure 1 was taken prior to conservation treatment. In raking light, with the illumination from the left side and parallel to the picture plane, the cupped and cracked paint film is evident.

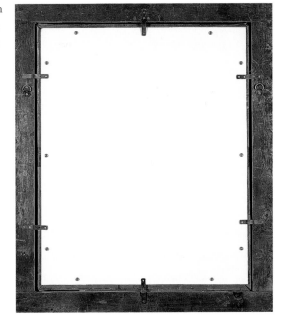

FIG. 6. (*right*) This image shows the reverse of a properly framed painting. Note the protective foam-board backing and brass mending plates and screws to attach the painting to the frame.

૭૧   *Treatment Procedures*

Conservators use a variety of procedures to stabilize paintings and attempt to return them to an appearance as close as possible to the artist's intention. The most urgent problems are structural ones, such as split wooden panels that need to be rejoined, torn fabrics that need mending, or lifted paint flakes that need to be flattened and re-adhered in a process called consolidation. Adhesives and small irons are used to reattach each flake in its proper position. Thin tissues and adhesives are used to bridge tears from behind and hold them in place.

Split wooden panels may require rejoining for structural security, but it is probably best to accept warping in a panel rather than to insist on flattening it. When a panel is warped, only thinning it will make it flexible enough to be flattened; numerous such treatments have resulted in the disastrous effect of inducing further splits. Wood needs to expand and contract with humidity fluctuations, and attempts to restrict movement are generally met with splits.

When fabric supports are torn, buckled, and weak, they can be flattened and reattached to the stretcher. When the support needs overall reinforcement, however, it can be lined onto an additional fabric support with an adhesive that is activated by heat. A heated table is used, and the painting is held under gentle vacuum pressure. Severely cupped and torn paintings may need to be lined onto solid support panels. Depending on the severity of damage and the sensitivity of the paint to heat and staining, adhesives used by conservators include thermoplastic resins and waxes.

Varnishes, especially natural resins, yellow over time and become grimy and dull. Unvarnished paint also attracts a grime film. Varnishes and grime should not be removed if the original paint will be damaged by cleaning agents. Sometimes varnish is selectively reduced if it cannot be evenly removed. After cleaning, a painting may be revarnished with a synthetic resin that will not yellow as readily as a natural resin film. While some conservators prefer the saturation of colors and the gloss of a natural resin film, synthetic varnishes can often be manipulated to match this appearance.

Missing areas of paint can be filled in with various puttylike materials and then textured and inpainted to match surrounding original paint. Cracks and stains can also be inpainted with nonyellowing, reversible synthetic paints. Conservators try to restrict such work to damaged areas only. The filling in of large areas of missing paint is done only if a reasonable assessment of the missing design can be made; otherwise, the newly painted area would be apparent to the viewer.

ઋ   *When to Call a Professional*

Proper treatment procedures to clean and stabilize paintings require a great deal of expertise; very few such procedures can be performed by someone other than a trained conservator. Perhaps because we are inundated with how-to information from books, television, and videos on everything from house remodeling to furniture repair, many people feel confident in attempting to clean and repair their own paintings. This almost always results in damage to the artwork. Delicate paint surfaces can be instantly and severely damaged by untrained persons who attempt to clean a painting with household cleaning products. Cleaning materials sold in art stores to "restore" and "revive" paintings contain strong solvents, which can dissolve paint, and coating materials, which may become unremovable in the future. Individuals who might never attempt to paint a picture on their own might be tempted to clean a painting due to the perceived familiarity of the task and kinship with household cleaning. Household detergents, soaps, and solvents can easily dissolve paint; water may also damage paint and can seep through cracks and wet the fabric support, causing it to shrink and paint layers to flake off. Even cleaning materials and methods that are accepted by conservators can be damaging when attempted by untrained hands.

Do not attempt to varnish a painting, as you may trap dirt under the varnish and complicate future cleaning efforts by a professional. Do not attempt to patch tears in a fabric support, thereby risking puckering and distortion. Finally, do not attempt to re-adhere flaking paint with glues, as this undermines procedures undertaken by conservators.

Do consult a conservation professional whenever a painting needs repair or cleaning. Even the most dirty, darkened, flaking painting can be stabilized, thereby preventing further damage. Owners of such forlorn paintings frequently are amazed by the bright color and detail that are revealed when the paintings are properly treated *(fig. 7)*.

ỡ   *Protecting Our Heritage*

Responding to criticisms of his experimental and often unstable painting techniques, eighteenth-century English painter Sir Joshua Reynolds once remarked, "All good pictures crack." They also buckle, warp, and fade; much of this is inevitable and irreversible. However, with proper care and a stable environment, most paintings can be maintained in a secure condition and enjoyed by future generations. We are entrusted with their care, and by making sound and informed decisions about conservation, we participate in the preservation of the artist's legacy.

FIG. 7. In this detail of *THOMAS WATLINGTON,* the discolored varnish has been partially removed from the painting, revealing the much brighter colors of the original design, still well preserved.

Furniture

MICHAEL S. PODMANICZKY

$\mathcal{T}$he idea of applying conservation principles to furniture is a relatively recent one. Only in the latter part of the twentieth century has furniture come to be considered "worthy" of such efforts. With six- and seven-figure prices not uncommon for high-end furniture and an ever-increasing regard for dearly loved family heirlooms, sound preservation and restoration techniques have never been more important. A solid understanding of materials and construction techniques is an essential foundation for the care and conservation of furniture.

◌ *Nature of the Materials*

Furniture conservation is divided into two general areas: structure and finish. Structure is further divided into solid, joined, and veneered wood. Finish can be painted or transparent (or in some cases both).

Problems with both structure and finish can be caused by abuse or misuse or may simply be the result of the natural aging process. Such aging includes both the consequences of normal, everyday wear and tear as well as the inevitable but natural deterioration of component materials themselves, which is referred to as *inherent vice*. Furniture commonly exhibits the effects of inherent vice, in which the qualities of materials or the manufacturing techniques may promote or be subject to deterioration merely through contact with one another or with the surrounding environment.

A better understanding of the materials used in furniture will help the owner/collector anticipate problems and provide the best environment for long-term care and preservation.

~ Structure

Wood is an anisotropic material, which simply means that its properties and strengths differ depending on how the wood is oriented. For example, wood is much stronger when the grain direction follows the longest dimension of a piece. As anyone who has chopped firewood knows, wood is easily split from the ends of a short log; it is impossible, however, to split crosswise—against the grain. If a piece of furniture is made with the wood grain oriented in a weak direction (because of style, design, or poor choice by the craftsman), damage may be encouraged.

Wood actively responds to the surrounding environment. It picks up moisture from the air and swells on days of high relative humidity and shrinks on dry days. When this happens, the anisotropic nature of wood is further illustrated; dimensional changes will occur across the grain only. For example, a solid wood table top will become slightly wider on very humid days but not measurably longer. Conversely, dry weather will cause wood to shrink across its width, but the length will remain constant. It is easy to imagine what happens if two pieces of wood are joined with the grain of one piece set at ninety degrees to the other. When the movement of one piece of wood is restricted by another, serious damage can occur (*fig. 1*).

~ Joined Wood

Because wood has maximum strength in one direction only, it is necessary to join many pieces in many directions to produce a strong, yet lightweight, three-dimensional object. For example, in a chair, legs are set with the grain in a vertical direction, but they are joined to horizontal seat rails that can withstand the weight of a sitter. Vertically set splats or horizontal rungs are oriented so that the strong grain direction takes the force of use. Although it is possible to so abuse a piece of fur-

FIG. 1. The desk-and-bookcase shown here has a severe crack that is wider at the bottom than at the top. The heavy base molding, which is attached across the grain of the wood in the side panel, kept the wood nearby from moving when there was a fluctuation in humidity. This caused a wide crack in the wood closest to the molding. However, the wood that is farther up the side and not constrained by the molding was allowed to move with fluctuations in humidity and therefore did not split as badly.

niture that these individual elements simply break across the grain, it is more common for failure to occur at the interface, or joint, between two parts.

To join two pieces of wood, it is necessary to cut away material from each to make the joint. Cutting away of any material, however, unavoidably weakens individual elements; it is at these interfaces that furniture is most vulnerable *(fig. 2)*.

Veneer

For centuries, expensive and highly figured wood has been cut into thin sheets and applied to more common, inexpensive "secondary" woods to create strikingly beau-

FIG. 2. The leg of this chair broke along the grain. A weak point in any chair occurs where three parts are joined in close proximity. Cutting joints into the top of the leg so that it fits into the seat rails weakens the wood; a break that begins in that area will extend into the solid area of the leg.

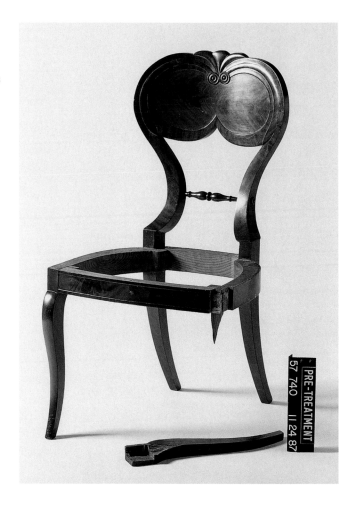

tiful furniture. This process is called *veneering*. In cases where plain veneer is used in full sheets that completely cover the secondary wood, the motivation is usually to reduce cost. However, veneer work often incorporates inlaid designs that can be simple or as exuberant and fanciful as French marquetry. The easiest way to think of marquetry is as a thin jigsaw puzzle that has been glued down to a wood base. Depending on how it is oriented, veneer work can be an example of cross-grain construction, which often results in the veneer being loosened or torn apart by unequal movement of the solid wood layers below *(fig. 3)*.

Traditional veneering involved water-based animal glue, which is subject to heat and moisture damage. Further damage can also be caused by humidity-related movement of the various wood components.

ை   Adhesives

The glue favored throughout history has been hot animal "hide" glue—with a consistency not unlike the substance that gels on the top of chilled, homemade soup or that serves as the basis for gelatin desserts. Extracted from skin, bones, and hooves, the glue is refined in a wide range of strengths for everything from food supplements to bookbinding adhesive.

Hide glue is purchased in dry, granular form; soaked in water; and melted at approximately 160°F. It is applied quickly, and the wood is joined before the temperature drops and causes it to gel; it is then left to dry. Under reasonably good conditions, hide glue can remain strong and effective for centuries. However, extreme moisture conditions can cause it to soften—resulting in joint or veneer problems—and very dry conditions can cause it to desiccate, or dry up, and crumble under stress.

ை   Finish

Until the end of the eighteenth century, a variety of natural resins, oils, and waxes were used to finish furniture. The resins were of two general classes: those that would easily dissolve in a solvent at room temperature (spirit varnishes) and those that needed to be heated to a very high temperature in linseed oil to dissolve and

FIG. 3. This card table is constructed of a soft-wood core that has been assembled in the same manner as a paneled door. It was then covered with a sheet of mahogany veneer. The movement of these core elements in response to changes in humidity has caused the veneer to detach at the corner and resulted in a tear at one of the joints in the soft-wood–core panel.

then be thinned in a solvent when cooled (oil resin varnishes). At the end of the century, shellac, a spirit varnish dissolved in alcohol, became the most common finish of choice. The quick evaporation of alcohol allowed shellac to be rubbed or wiped, rather than brushed, onto furniture in a process commonly referred to as French polishing. This eliminated brushstrokes and other imperfections and greatly speeded up the finishing process.

Beeswax dissolved in turpentine and linseed oil, thinned in the same solvent, were both used as finishing materials on a limited basis; neither forms a durable film. By saturating the wood surface, its color could be enhanced, but protection from stains, water, and wear was minimal.

Stains or other colorants were often used to enhance the appearance of fine furniture during the finishing process. Traditional materials were generally divided into two groups: pigments (small particles from mineral sources) and dyes (coloring matter extracted from natural plant sources). Dyes were desirable because they are more transparent than pigments; however, they are also more prone to fading from exposure to light. It was only toward the end of the nineteenth century that synthetic dyes of somewhat greater light-fastness were developed, although even the most colorfast dyes today are susceptible to light fading.

๏   *What You Can Do*

Unequal wood movement in response to relative humidity changes, an unavoidable inherent vice, can be one of the most significant causes of damage to furniture and other wood objects. When wood elements are assembled to form a three-dimensional object, each element responds to humidity in a different direction, depending on its orientation.

Ideally, furniture should be kept at a reasonably constant relative humidity, in the general range of 50 percent. However, some homeowners do not have sophisticated climate controls and are unable to provide more than rudimentary defense for their objects.

Forced-air heat can create extremely dry conditions during winter months and can damage a normally "healthy" piece of furniture. There are a few things you can do to prolong the life of your favorite pieces. Keep furniture away from the direct impact of dry, forced air. A humidifier can certainly help minimize the overall fluctuation of environmental moisture by controlling relative humidity changes. Be aware, however, that once wood has deformed or split because of radical moisture change, it is impossible to return it to its original state. Although a professional conservator will be able to offer passive approaches aimed at minimizing further deterioration and maximizing long-term strength and stability, the best care is preventive care, which means environmental control.

๑ Light

Color fading is another example of an inherent vice. It is a problem for furniture because of the susceptibility of stains and the color of wood itself to both natural and artificial light damage *(fig. 4)*. Although not as serious as the fading of the wood color itself, natural finishes will also begin to deteriorate over time when exposed to light. As with any material that is subject to light damage, fine furniture should be kept away from direct sunlight to preserve color and finish. Ultraviolet filters on windows can provide a useful defense against the damaging effects of light.

๑ General Cleaning

To properly care for furniture that is stable and has a sound finish, little more than gentle cleaning and waxing is necessary. Everyday cleaning can usually be limited

FIG. 4. The natural colors of wood, stain, and finish are unstable in the presence of all light ranges, particularly ultraviolet light. Often fading, darkening, or color shifts happen so slowly that they are not immediately noticeable. This table shows the effects of light damage and illustrates the importance of protecting objects from both sunlight and fluorescent lighting. Objects were placed on the table and left there for some time. In addition, the leaf was folded down and was exposed more directly to sunlight from a nearby window. Both circumstances resulted in a noticeable contrast between the exposed and the shielded areas of the table.

to dusting with a soft cotton cloth or brush. A dust-attracting commercial aerosol, lightly sprayed onto the cloth rather than on the furniture, will help in picking up surface dust from broad, flat areas. For carved details or other areas where dusting with a cloth is impractical, a soft brush, such as a woman's cosmetic brush, is useful. Feather dusters should be avoided. They may start out feeling soft, but they quickly lose that softness; the stiff middle rib of the feathers can also scratch finishes.

Gentle cleaning begins with a mild detergent and water. Detergents work as bridges between oily dirt and water so that dirt can be lifted away by the water. A current example of a mild detergent is a Kodak photographic product sold under the name "Photo-Flo." Photo-Flo is similar to the types of detergents favored by conservators and is readily available from any photographic supply house. Typically, a few drops of a mild detergent in a quart of water is sufficient. Dampen a soft cotton cloth with this solution, and lightly wipe the surface of the object, turning the cloth as it becomes soiled. Cotton swabs can be used to clean carved areas or detailed moldings. Go over the piece a second time with a clean cloth that is dampened in water alone.

Next, a solvent may be necessary to remove soiling that is left behind by water-based cleaning. "Odorless" paint thinner is a mild solvent that is unlikely to damage a sound finish. Wet a cotton swab, and rub a small, out-of-the-way area for a few seconds. Observe the finish for any signs of damage, and feel the surface to see if it has become sticky, indicating that it is being dissolved by the paint thinner. Stop immediately if this happens. If there is no damage, dampen a cloth with the solvent, and repeat the cleaning process as indicated above. Only a conservator should attempt to remove the serious buildup of material on an old finish or an old finish that has started to crack, separate, or otherwise deteriorate.

ꙮ   *Fixing Scratches*

If there are superficial scratches in the finish, they can often be hidden by saturating them with a very thin application of shellac. Commercial shellac should be thinned 50/50 with denatured alcohol and applied with a fine, pointed artist's watercolor brush. If the scratch still shows, watercolor or artist's acrylic paints can be mixed to match the color of the finish. These paints can also be applied with a fine-point brush, followed by a sealing coat of thinned shellac. Whenever a brushstroke of finish is applied to a surface, there is the danger that it will exhibit "tide lines," or ridges, at the edges. By thinning the shellac and carefully applying it to the damaged area only, this danger is minimized.

When the surface is completely dry and touch-ups are complete, apply a paste wax according to instructions on the can. Paste wax, often referred to as "butcher's wax," is a mix of plant- and beeswax with turpentine, which is used as a softening solvent. Wax is a stable, chemically inert material that is an excellent dust and water repellent and is easily removed and replaced. Paste wax can be clear (white) or various shades of brown. Light-color furniture should be waxed with clear paste; brown wax is preferred for dark furniture.

The turpentine solvent in paste wax is an excellent cleaning solvent. Often, rewaxing is all that is necessary to keep the surface of furniture clean, protected, and looking its best. For furniture that does not receive much use, waxing once or twice a year should be adequate. However, with heavy use it may be necessary to wax as often as once a month.

ﾌ Broken or Loose Pieces

Small or minor loose pieces of carving or veneer can easily be reattached. Hot hide glue is available through most woodworking catalogues, but a reasonable substitute is animal glue that has been liquefied and then treated to keep it from gelling during the setting process. This glue is mixed with chemicals so that it remains in a liquid state. It comes in plastic squeeze bottles and is available at most hardware stores. Many conservators feel that this glue is not as strong as the real thing and therefore do not recommend it for major structural repairs.

Repairing veneer can be as simple as re-gluing the loose piece of veneer or inlay. However, the process may be complicated by the need to glue into areas that are nearly inaccessible. Conservators and restorers often employ syringes to inject glue under a split or lifted edge. If this is not possible, the veneer can be carefully split along the grain with a razor blade to deliver glue exactly where needed. Pressing the veneer or inlay flat is crucial, so a selection of clamps with wood or plastic pads (to protect against damaging the veneer) is essential.

When repairing any break (especially breaks in solid wood), proper alignment of the break is critical for a satisfactory repair. If adhesives are introduced into the interface of a break and that break is not properly aligned, it will be necessary to redo the repair. If the adhesive is not easily reversible, further damage can occur. So-called hot melt glues, delivered with an electric gunlike dispenser and often used for crafts projects, are bulky and tend not to squeeze out of joints, virtually ensuring a misaligned repair.

Most modern adhesives are manufactured to resist reversibility and, therefore, create conservation problems if they are not used creatively. Avoid epoxy or polyester adhesives that use a catalyst and carpenter's "white" and "yellow" glues. None of these can easily be redissolved if future problems arise.

১   *Important Points*

- When cleaning furniture, it is important to avoid wetting the surface heavily, since too much exposure to moisture may damage the finish.

- Most finishes will dissolve in a strong solvent, so anything stronger than paint thinner, such as fingernail polish remover (acetone) or lacquer thinner, should be avoided when cleaning or touching up.

- Do not attempt to use steel wool to "polish" a surface, either by itself or with a solvent. Steel wool is a fine abrasive and, like sandpaper, will leave scratches in the surface.

- Many commercial polishes are ineffective or potentially damaging to fine furniture finishes. For example, silicon-based polishes provide an immediate gloss, but silicon residue—either on the surface or, more seriously, in cracks and fissures—will inhibit future treatment of the finish.

১

There is no mystery to caring for and preserving the historic, aesthetic, personal, and monetary value of furniture—nor are the principles involved difficult to understand. Owners play an integral part in providing a healthy environment and maintaining the cleanliness and appearance of their objects. Minor repairs, as discussed above, are well within the capability of most owners. However, when structural or finish problems are not easily addressed or the piece that is involved is of historical significance, a professional conservator should always be consulted.

CHAPTER 12

Gilded Frames

MICHAEL S. PODMANICZKY AND MARY C. PETERSON

For years, gilded frames have been considered works of art in themselves. Gilded frames of the eighteenth and nineteenth centuries are made of wood. Such frames were hand-cut using a shaped plane, and ornamentation was either carved directly into the wood or applied separately. Applied elements could be made of wood or a plasticlike composition called *compo*. Compo is a mixture of powdered chalk, animal glue, natural resin, and linseed oil that acts very much like bread dough and is easily pressed into carved wooden molds. When set, it becomes hard and durable. Compo elements are often mistaken for plaster. Large, deep frames were often created with several pieces of molding that were joined with glue, nails, wooden pegs, or splines. In ornate frames the ornamentation often concealed joins at the corners.

As with furniture, many styles of frames were veneered. Paint was occasionally applied, but the surface treatment most commonly associated with frames is gold leaf. In fact, the care of picture frames is largely the care of gilded surfaces, which are created with their own special materials and techniques.

The Nature of Gilding

To create a gilded surface on frames, a coating of diluted animal glue is applied over the wood, and then many layers of gesso are applied until an even surface is achieved. The layer that is applied on top of the gesso is known as *bole*—a mixture of clay and animal glue that is similar to gesso but harder. Gold leaf is then adhered by wetting the bole to momentarily reactivate the animal glue or by coating the bole with a type of varnish to which the gold leaf will stick *(fig. 1)*. The former is referred to as *water gilding*, and the latter is known as *oil gilding* (from the linseed oil that is a component of the varnish). Despite similarities in appearance, water gilding and oil gilding present two entirely different types of surfaces for care or repair.

Some gilded surfaces are oil-gilded directly onto painted or varnished picture frames, with no gesso layers. In these cases, the gilding can be treated much like another coat of paint or varnish. A final coating referred to as a *toner* is then often applied to soften the appearance of the gold. The toner can be a variety of resins,

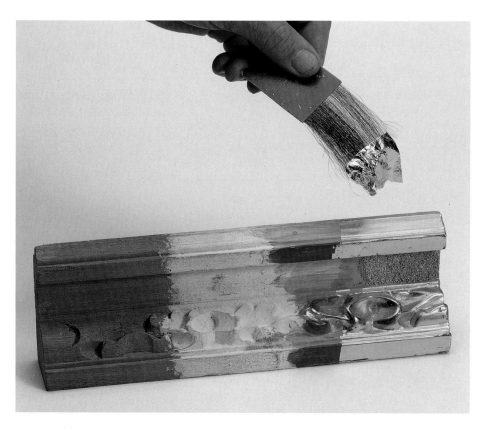

FIG. 1. Gilding is composed of many layers. Starting with a bare wood, a coating of animal glue is applied, then the surface is filled with gold leaf. Gold leaf is extremely thin and delicate. Even a breath of air before it has adhered to the wood can damage it severly.

often dissolved in alcohol and carefully brushed or wiped on. The toner layer is generally quite fragile and easily damaged.

Although actual gold leaf is the most prized material for gilding, silver leaf or even copper or bronze powders can be used to simulate the look of gold or create exciting variations in the appearance of the gilded surface. In many cases, the frames we see today are frames that either have been reworked with overgilding (using oil size, or, in rare instances, water gilding) or have been painted to simulate gold. The type of paint used can vary widely; many products are available commercially. Once they are used on frames, they are easily detected: bronze powder paints or "radiator" paint will tarnish and darken. Gold leaf will not, although the toning layer can attract dirt and grease and become darkened over time.

Care of Gilded Frames

Because of the ephemeral nature of gilding, many gold-leaf frames from the eighteenth and nineteenth centuries have not survived well, or at all. In caring for such frames, there are numerous factors that you must consider. First, discover what type of gilding is present—water gilding or oil gilding. That fact will determine the care strategy. Water gilding is easily damaged by moisture, so typical water-based cleaning solutions should be avoided, as should direct contact with water. Where oil gilding is encountered without any animal-glue ground, the gilding is not as threatened by moisture.

General Cleaning

If you are in doubt about the material makeup of your frame, consult a conservator or reputable restorer who can help you identify what materials are present, the extent of damage, and whether the task is one that you should undertake or leave to a professional. Once the materials are known, the proper aqueous or nonaqueous cleaning solutions can be chosen. The conservator can guide you in making that choice.

In cleaning a gilded frame, start with the least-invasive solution. To avoid removing the gilding along with the grime, test a small area first (no larger than the head of a cotton swab). Dip a cotton swab in the appropriate solution, squeeze dry, and lightly roll the swab over the test spot. You may see only a slight discoloration on the swab; this means that the solution is working. Proceed slowly in small areas, and retest any parts that have a different finish.

If chemical solvents are required to remove paint layers, it is not recommended that you attempt this at home. Knowing the correct solvent to accomplish the job requires careful testing by someone who is familiar with the reactions of the chemicals. A solvent that removes grime on one part of a frame may be destructive to another part.

Running a dust cloth over gilding will, in time, remove the toner and the gold leaf. Minimal, but usually adequate, care for picture frames should be limited to dusting with a brush, such as those used to apply makeup *(fig. 2)*.

Fɪɢ. 2. General maintenance of a gilded frame should be limited to gentle dusting with a soft brush. If a gilded surface is flaking or chipping, brushing will aggravate the situation. In such cases, a conservator should be consulted.

≈ *Heat and Humidity*

As with all wood objects, changes in temperature and humidity will cause frame parts to expand and contract. On gilded frames, the gesso layers and the compo will react differently to humidity than will the wood, resulting in surface cracks and flaking of the gold leaf and ornamentation. Frames should not be hung or stored near sources of heat or in areas with fluctuating temperature and humidity (attics and basements).

Damage to a frame's wood and compo can be repaired with the same adhesives that are used on furniture. However, because of the many different materials used to produce a gilded surface, treatment should be undertaken only by a trained professional.

≈ *Structural Damage*

The most common structural problem with frames is the separating of miters, at the corners. If this occurs, loose nails at the joint can be tapped back into place. To do so, place the frame on a table with padding. Using a hammer and a small nail set (available at any hardware store), tap all four corners until the miters close. If possible, add animal or wood glue to the miter and clamp lightly. Be sure to pad the frame sides so that the finish is not damaged.

Because of the sensitivity of gilded objects to a wide range of solvents as well as to water, the care of these objects must be restrained. Any treatment of a gilded object beyond what is outlined above should be undertaken only by a professional conservator.

RESOURCES

PROFESSIONAL ORGANIZATIONS

AMERICAN INSTITUTE FOR CONSERVATION OF
HISTORIC AND ARTISTIC WORKS (AIC)
1717 K Street NW, Suite 200
Washington, DC 20036
202-452-9545

AMERICAN ASSOCIATION OF MUSEUMS (AAM)
1575 Eye Street NW, Suite 400
Washington, DC 20005-1113
202-289-1818

INTERNATIONAL INSTITUTE FOR CONSERVATION
OF HISTORIC AND ARTISTIC WORKS (IIC)
6 Buckingham Street
London WC2N 6BA
UK
01-839-5975

CANADIAN ASSOCIATION FOR CONSERVATION
(CAC)
280 Metcalfe Street, Suite 400
Ottawa, Canada
K2P 1R7

THE AMERICAN INSTITUTE FOR CONSERVATION OF HISTORIC AND ARTISTIC WORKS (AIC) is the national membership organization of conservation professionals dedicated to preserving art and historic artifacts and promoting public understanding of the role that conservation of such objects plays in preserving our cultural heritage. The AICs Guide to Conservation Services is available free to private individuals interested in locating a conservator. By simply providing a complete description of the object needing treatment, the type of conservation service required, and the geographic region in which you prefer to have the work done, you will be sent the brochure "Guidelines for Selecting a Conservator," along with a computer-generated list of AIC member conservators.

For more information about AIC services, call 202-452-9545 or write AMERICAN INSTITUTE FOR CONSERVATION, 1717 K Street NW, Suite 200, Washington, DC 20036. You can visit their web site at http://aic.stanford.edu/ or request additional information via email at info@aic-faic.org.

INSTITUTIONS WITH ANALYTICAL FACILITIES

CANADIAN CONSERVATION INSTITUTE
1030 Innes Road
Ottawa, ONT, Canada
K1A 0M5
613.998.3721 ext. 406
www.cci-icc.gc.ca

CARNEGIE MELLON RESEARCH INSTITUTE
700 Technology Drive
Box 2950
Pittsburgh, PA 15230-2950
412.268.3100
www.cmu.edu/cmri

DETROIT INSTITUTE OF ARTS
Conservation Services Lab
5200 Woodward Avenue
Detroit, MI 48202
313.833.7900
www.dia.org

FREER GALLERY OF ART
Smithsonian Institution
Jefferson Drive at 12th Street, SW
Washington, DC 20560
202.357.4880
www.si.edu/organiza/museums/freer

GETTY CONSERVATION INSTITUTE
1200 Getty Center Drive, Suite 700
Los Angeles, CA 90049-1684
310.440.7300
www.getty.edu/gci

LOS ANGELES COUNTY MUSEUM OF ART
5905 Wilshire Boulevard
Los Angeles, CA 90036
323.857.6000
www.lacma.org

MCCRONE RESEARCH INSTITUTE
2820 South Michigan Avenue
Chicago, IL 60616
312.842.7100
www.mcri.org

METROPOLITAN MUSEUM OF ART
Sherman Fairchild Center for Object
Conservation
1000 Fifth Avenue
New York, NY 10028-0198
212.535.7710
www.metmuseum.org

MUSEUM APPLIED SCIENCE CENTER FOR
ARCHAEOLOGY
The University Museum of Archaeology and
Anthropology
University of Pennsylvania
33rd and Spruce Streets
Philadelphia, PA 19104-6324
215.898.4001
www.upenn.edu/museum

MUSEUM OF FINE ARTS
Objects Conservation and Scientific Research
465 Huntington Avenue
Boston, MA 02115
617.267.9300
www.mfa.org

MUSEUM OF MODERN ART
Conservation Department
11 West 53rd Street
New York, NY 10019
212.708.9400
www.moma.org

NATIONAL ARCHIVES
8601 Adelphi Road
College Park, MD 20740
800.234.8861
www.nara.gov

NATIONAL GALLERY OF ART
Conservation Division
6th and Constitution Avenue, NW
Washington, DC 20565
202.737.4215
www.nga.gov

NATIONAL PARK SERVICE
Harpers Ferry Center
P.O Box 50
Harpers Ferry, WV 25425
304.535.6211
www.nps.gov

PHILADELPHIA MUSEUM OF ART
Conservation Department
PO Box 7646
Philadelphia, PA 19101-7646
215.763.8100
www.pma.libertynet.org

SMITHSONIAN CENTER FOR MATERIALS
RESEARCH AND EDUCATION
Smithsonian Institution
Museum Support Center
4210 Silver Hill Road
Suitland, MD 20746
301.238.3700
www.si.edu/scmre

STRAUS CENTER FOR CONSERVATION
Harvard University Art Museums
32 Quincy Street
Cambridge, MA 02138
617.495.2392
www.artmuseums.harvard.edu/strausmain.html

WILLIAMSTOWN ART CONSERVATION
CENTER, INC.
225 South Street
Williamstown, MA 01267
413.458.5741
www.clark.williams.edu

WINTERTHUR MUSEUM, GARDEN & LIBRARY
Conservation Division
Winterthur, DE 19735
302.888.4600
www.winterthur.org

SELECTED LIST OF SUPPLIERS

ARCHIVAL PRODUCTS
P.O. Box 1413
Des Moines, IA 50305-1413
800.526.5640
800.262.4091 (fax)
e-mail: archival@ix.netcom.com
www.archival.com
Catalogue available
Archival paper, book, and storage supplies

ARCHIVART
Division of Heller & Usdan
7 Caesar Place
Moonachie, NJ 07074
800.804.8428
210.935.5964 (fax)
Archival paper, book, and storage supplies

BENCHMARK
P.O. Box 214
Rosemont, NJ 08556
609.397.1131
609.397.1159 (fax)
Catalogue available
*Archival paper, book, storage, and
exhibition supplies*

CONSERVATION RESOURCES
8888-H Forbes Place
Springfield, VA 22151
800.634.6932
703.321.0629 (fax)
Catalogue available
Archival paper, book, and storage supplies

CONSERVATORS EMPORIUM
100 Standing Rock Circle
Reno, NV 89511
702.852.0404
702.852.3737 (fax)
Archival paper, book, and storage supplies

CUSTOM MANUFACTURING, INC.
P.O. Box 1215
Emmitsburg, MD 21727
717.642.6304
717.642.6596 (fax)
Archival paper, book, and storage supplies

GAYLORD BROTHERS
Archival Division
P.O. Box 4901 Syracuse, NY 13221-14901
800.448.6160
800.272.3412 (fax)
www.gaylord.com
Catalogue, free pamphlets and conservation
help line (800.428.3831)
Archival paper, book, and storage supplies

Library Binding Institute
7401 Metro Blvd., Suite 325
Edina, MN 55439-3031
612.835.4707
612.835.4780 (fax)
e-mail: 71035.3504@compuserve.com
Archival paper, book, and storage supplies

Light Impressions
P.O. Box 940
Rochester, NY 14603-0940
800.828.6216
800.828.5539 (fax)
www.lightimpressionsdirect.com
Catalogue available
Archival paper, book, and storage supplies
Specialists in photography

Northeast Documents Conservation
Center
100 Brickstone Square
Andover, MA 01810-1494
508.470.1010
508.475.6021 (fax)
Archival paper, book, and storage supplies

Talas
568 Broadway, Suite 107
New York, NY 10012
212.219.0770
212.219.0735 (fax)
Catalogue available
Archival paper, book, and storage supplies

Testfabrics, Inc.
415 Delaware Avenue
P.O. Box 26
West Pittston, PA 18643
570.603.0432
507.603.0433 (fax)
Archival textile supplies

Troy Mills
18 Monadnock Street
Troy, NY 03465-1000
603.242.7711
Archival textile supplies

University Products, Inc.
Archival Division
517 Main Street, P.O. Box 101
Holyoke, MA 01041-0101
800.628.1912
800.532.9281 (fax)
www.universityproducts.com
Catalogue available
Archival paper, book, and storage supplies

SUGGESTED READINGS

Applebaum, Barbara. *Guide to Environmental Protection of Collections*. Madison, Conn.: Sound View Press, 1991.

Bachmann, Konstanze, ed. *Conservation Concerns: A Guide for Collectors and Curators*. Washington, D.C.: Smithsonian Institution Press, 1992.

Baldwin, Gordon. *Looking at Photographs: A Guide to Technical Terms*. Malibu, Calif.: J. Paul Getty Museum, 1991.

Ellis, Margaret H. *The Care of Prints and Drawings*. Nashville: American Association for State and Local History, 1987.

MacLeish, Bruce A. *The Care of Antiques and Historical Collections*. Nashville: American Association for State and Local History, 1985.

McGiffen, Robert F. Jr. *Furniture Care and Conservation*. Nashville: American Association for State and Local History, 1983.

National Committee to Save America's Cultural Collections. *Caring for Your Collections*. New York: Harry N. Abrams, 1992.

Ogden, Sherelyn, ed. *Preservation of Library and Archival Materials*. Andover, Mass.: Northeast Document Center, 1994.

Reilly, James M. *Care and Identification of Nineteenth-Century Photographic Prints*. Kodak Publication G-2S. Rochester, N.Y.: Eastman Kodak Co., 1986.

Sandwith, Hermione, and Sheila Stainton, *The National Trust Manual of Housekeeping*. Middlesex, Eng.: Viking Penguin, 1985.

Shelley, Marjorie. *The Care and Handling of Art Objects*. New York: Metropolitan Museum of Art, 1987.

Thomson, Garry. *The Museum Environment*. London: Butterworths, 1986.

SELECTED WEB SITES

www.pch.gc.ca
   Canadian Conservation Institute

www.cr.nps.gov/csd/publications
   Conserve O Gram, National Parks Service Museum Management Program

www.aic.stanford.edu
   American Institute for Conservation

www.art_restoration.com
   New Orleans Conservation Guild

www.du.edu/rmcc
   Rocky Mountain Conservation Center

LIST OF ILLUSTRATIONS

CHAPTER 3: *Books, Manuscripts, and Ephemera*

FIG. 1.
Assemblage of books, manuscripts, paper dolls, maps, and miscellaneous ephemera

FIG. 2.
Demonstration of proper method of photocopying bound materials

FIG. 3.
Demonstration of proper method of turning pages in a book; depiction of support necessary to reduce risk of damage to bindings, particulary in large books

FIG. 4.
Properly and improperly shelved books

FIG. 5.
Book boxes and enclosures

FIG. 6.
Archival-quality boxes, folders, and plastic sleeves for storing manuscripts and printed ephemera

FIG. 7.
Demonstration of preparing a blueprint or other large printed piece for safe storage

CHAPTER 4: *Organic Materials*

FIG. 1.7
DOLL
United States, nineteenth century
Corn husk, paint
H. 8", W. 3 $1/2$"
64.873 Bequest of Henry Francis du Pont

FIG. 2.
Doll displayed on proper stand

FIG. 3.
FIRE BUCKET
United States, 1776
Vegetable-tanned leather, bast fibers, paint
H. 19 $3/4$", Diam. 9 $1/4$"
60.722 Bequest of Henry Francis du Pont

FIG. 4.
Parts of fire bucket's original handle

FIG. 5.
Left: DICE CUP
Probably England, nineteenth century
Bone
H. 3 $7/8$", Diam. 1 $3/4$"
65.633.2 Bequest of Henry Francis du Pont

Right: SEAL
Probably England, 1795–1825
Ivory, copper alloy
H. 3 $5/8$", W. 1 $5/8$"
58.2588 Bequest of Henry Francis du Pont

FIG. 6.
BOX
Probably England, 1715–55
Walnut burl, tortoiseshell, silver
H. 1 $5/8$", W. 3 $5/8$", L. 6 $1/4$"
59.2578 Bequest of Henry Francis du Pont

FIG. 7.
Open view of box (fig. 6)

FIG. 8.
Background: BATTLEDORE
England, 1816–25
Wood, oil-tanned leather, vellum, gilt
H. 17 $1/4$", W. 5 $1/2$", Diam. $3/4$"
58.1794.3 Bequest of Henry Francis du Pont

Foreground: SHUTTLECOCKS
Europe, ca. 1850
Feathers, cork, leather, silk velvet, cotton with brass threads
H. 4", W. 3 $5/8$"
54.71.2, .3 Gift of Henry Francis du Pont

CHAPTER 5: *Ceramics and Glass*

FIG. 1.
PLATE
Ralph Clews (signed), Staffordshire, Eng.,
1819–34
Earthenware
Diam. 9 1/8"
61.439.2 Gift of the J. W. Webb family

FIG. 2.
SWEETMEAT DISH
Dagoty & Honore, Paris, 1817
Porcelain
W. 8 3/4"
58.1606.50 Bequest of Henry Francis du Pont

FIG. 3.
DRINKING GLASS
H. 3 1/2"
Teaching collection, Winterthur/University of
Delaware Program in Art Conservation

FIG. 4.
DISH
Pennsylvania, 1800–1875
Redware/earthenware
L. 12 3/4", W. 8 3/4"
67.1793 Bequest of Henry Francis du Pont

FIG. 5.
TUREEN AND COVER
(smiling Buddha; Pu-Tai Ho-Shang)
China, 1760–70
Porcelain
H. 14"
96.4.97 Campbell Collection of Soup Tureens
at Winterthur, Gift of Mrs. Elinor Dorrance
Ingersoll

FIG. 6.
TUREEN AND COVER (fig. 5) in UV light

CHAPTER 6: *Textiles*

FIG. 1.
UPHOLSTERY FABRIC
France, 1750–75
Polychrome warp-compound weave with stripes
and floral sprigs in pink, blue, and light green
H. 31 3/4", W. 22 3/4"
69.5076 Bequest of Henry Francis du Pont

FIG. 2.
Vacuum cleaner with attachment to control
suction; screening bound at edges with cotton
twill tape

FIG. 3.
PIECED QUILT
Rebecca Scattergood Savery, Philadelphia, 1827
Cotton
H. 31 3/4", W. 22 3/4"
97.22 Museum purchase with funds provided
by the Estate of Mrs. Samuel Pettit and additional funds by Mr. Samuel Pettit in memory of
his wife

FIG. 4.
Small textile mount revealing tripartite assemblage: (1) acid-free board covered with (2) nee-
dle-
punched polyester felt and (3) a finish fabric

FIG. 5.
NEEDLEWORK
Catherine Skinner Ward, Philadelphia, 1816
Silk, linen, watercolors
H. 18 3/8", W. 25 1/4"
91.46 Museum purchase

FIG. 6.
Reverse of textile with hook-and-loop
fastener

FIG. 7.
DOLL
Probably Philadelphia, 1835–45
Cotton, silk, leather, composition, human hair
H. 21"
91.23 Gift of Ruth Young Buggy in memory of
Caroline Bacon Willoughby Young

CHAPTER 7: *Photographs*

FIG. 1.
Leather photograph case with ambrotype (*left*)
and daguerreotype (*right*)
ca. 1860
Images: H. 3 $1/4$", W. 2 $1/2$"; case (closed)
H. 3 $1/2$", W. 3 $1/8$"
Private collection

FIG. 2.
TINTYPES
1860s–1885
H. 3 $1/2$", W. 2 $1/2$"
Private collection

FIG. 3.
Albumen prints in cartes-de-visite format
1860–70
H. 2 $1/2$", W. 4"
Private collection

FIG. 4.
Silver gelatin photographs
1910–40
Private collection

FIG.5.
Products of the varied nineteenth-century print
processes
Private collection

FIG.6.
Cased daguerreotypes and ambrotypes
H. 3$1/2$", W. 3$1/8$"
Private collection

CHAPTER 8: *Metals*

FIG. 1.
TUREEN, COVER, AND STAND
Robert Garrard Jr., London, 1824–25
Silver
H. 15 $11/16$", L. 21", W. 15 $1/2$"
96.4.254 Campbell Collection of Soup Tureens
at Winterthur

FIG. 2.
Left: OPIUM LAMP
China, 1800–1830
Enamel on copper, glass
H. 4 $3/4$", W. 3 $3/8$"
64.81 Gift of J. A. Lloyd Hyde

Center: ARGAND LAMP
Baldwin Gardiner (also Thomas Messenger and
Sons), London, 1827–46
Copper alloy, iron, glass
H. 20 $3/4$", W. 18 $3/8$"
76.195.1 Gift of Charles van Ravenswaay

Right: BOX
United States., 1825–60
Iron, tin, copper alloy, paint, lacquer
L. 8 $1/2$", H. 5 $1/4$", Diam. 3 $3/4$"
67.820 Bequest of Henry Francis du Pont

FIG. 3.
Left: SPOON
James Yates, Birmingham, Eng., 1800–1840
Pewter/Britannia
L 4 $15/16$", W. $15/16$"
65.277.2 Bequest of Henry Francis du Pont

Right: BELL
United States, 1750–1850
Silver
H. 5"
64.53 Gift of the Historical Society of
Pennsylvania

CHAPTER 9: *Works of Art on Paper*

CHAPTER 10: *Paintings*

Fɪɢ. 2.
Schematic illustration of the layered structure
of a painting on fabric, showing the stretcher,
support fabric, ground, paint, and varnish
Drawing, Mark F. Bockrath

Fɪɢ. 3.
MARY NORMAN ROSE PRINCE (detail)
United States, ca. 1820
Oil on fabric
H. 20", W. 17" (oval)
98.1679 Museum purchase with funds pro-
vided by Mrs. O. Ray Moore

Fɪɢ. 4.
LANDSCAPE (detail)
United States, nineteenth century
Oil on fabric
H. 10", W. 14"
Teaching collection, Winterthur/University of
Delaware Program in Art Conservation

Fɪɢ. 5.
Vɪᴇᴡ ᴏꜰ *THE PEACEABLE KINGDOM*
(fig.1) in raking light

Fɪɢ. 6.
Reverse of a properly framed painting

Fɪɢ. 7.
THOMAS WATLINGTON (detail)
ca. 1840
Oil on fabric
H. 28", W. 24"
Private collection

CHAPTER 11: *Furniture*

Fɪɢ. 1.
Sɪᴅᴇ ᴄʜᴀɪʀ
New York, 1825–40
Mahogany, ash, cherry
H. 34", W. 17 ³⁄₈", Diam. 18"
57.740.1 Bequest of Henry Francis du Pont

Fɪɢ. 2.
Cᴀʀᴅ ᴛᴀʙʟᴇ
Baltimore, 1800–1820
Tulip-poplar, pine, maple, mahogany veneer
H. 28 ⁵⁄₈", W. 36", Diam. 35 ³⁄₄"
57.1072.1 Bequest of Henry Francis du Pont

Fɪɢ. 3.
Dᴇsᴋ-ᴀɴᴅ-ʙᴏᴏᴋᴄᴀsᴇ
John Welch, Boston, 1743–48
Mahogany, sabicu, white pine, red cedar
H. 97 ¹⁄₄", W. 42 ⁷⁄₈", Diam. 23 ¹⁄₂"
60.1134 Gift of Henry Francis du Pont

Fɪɢ. 4.
Pᴇᴍʙʀᴏᴋᴇ ᴛᴀʙʟᴇ
John Dikeman
New York, 1795–1810
Mahogany, rosewood, chestnut, beech, pine,
white ash
H. 37 ¹⁄₂", W. 31", L. 37 ¹⁄₂"
57.1001.2 Bequest of Henry Francis du Pont

CHAPTER 12: *Gilded Frames*

Fɪɢ. 1.
Gilding process on partial wooden frame
Winterthur

Fɪɢ. 2.
Gentle dusting of gilded frame
Winterthur

ABOUT THE AUTHORS

*T*he following Winterthur staff members authored and contributed to *The Winterthur Guide to Caring for Your Collection*:

MARK F. BOCKRATH,
conservator of paintings

JANICE CARLSON,
senior scientist

KATE DUFFY,
associate scientist

LINDA EATON,
curator of textiles
(former conservator of textiles)

BETTY FISKE,
conservator of paper

ROBERT W. HOAG,
supervisor of collections maintenance

JOHN KRILL,
senior conservator of paper

GREGORY J. LANDREY,
senior conservator and director of the Conservation Division

MARGARET A. LITTLE,
associate conservator of objects

MARY C. PETERSON,
conservation assistant

MICHAEL S. PODMANICZKY,
senior conservator of furniture

BRUNO P. POULIOT,
associate conservator of objects

LOIS OLCOTT PRICE,
senior conservator of library collections

DEBRA HESS NORRIS is director of the Winterthur/University of Delaware Program in Art Conservation and associate professor of photograph conservation at the University of Delaware.

WINTERTHUR MUSEUM, GARDEN & LIBRARY is nestled in the beautiful Brandywine Valley, halfway between New York City and Washington, D.C. Home to the world's premier collection of early American decorative arts, a matchless twentieth-century naturalistic garden, and a world-renowned research library, the Winterthur estate is the former home of Henry Francis du Pont, an avid collector and horticulturist.

The highly trained conservation professionals at Winterthur work in one of the finest laboratory and research facilities in the United States. Their commitment to the preservation and conservation of art and historical works extends to teaching in an internationally recognized conservation program jointly sponsored by Winterthur and the University of Delaware. Begun in 1974, the Master's degree program in Art Conservation is one of only four such programs in the country.

To learn more about Winterthur, call 800.448.3883, 302.888.4600, or TDD 302.888.4907, or visit our web site at *www.winterthur.org*.